Jack and the Beanstalk

A Pantomime

John Morley

Samuel French – London

New York – Sydney – Toronto – Hollywood

ISBN 0 573 06463 6

CHARACTERS

Dame Trot
Jack, her son
Silly Billy, her other son
King Satupon
Princess Melanie, his daughter
Daisy, the Cow
Sergeant Spick } The King's Guardsmen
Corporal Span }
Clarence Clanger, the Town Crier

IMMORTALS
Fleshcreep, the Giant's Henchman
The Vegetable Fairy
The Dreaded Dragon
Giant Blunderbore
Mrs Blodwyn Blunderbore, his wife

Villagers, Townspeople, Magic Beanstalk People, Prisoners of the Giant, Wedding Guests

ACT I
Scene 1 The Village of Pennyfarthing
Scene 2 Outside Daisy's Cowshed in the Village
Scene 3 The Cattle Market in the nearby Town
Scene 4 On the way back to the Village
Scene 5 Inside Dame Trot's Cottage
Scene 6 Beanstalkland up in the Clouds

ACT II
Scene 1 The Dragon's Cave outside the Giant's Castle
Scene 2 The Henchman's evil Grotto in the Castle
Scene 3 The Giant's Kitchen
Scene 4 Down to Earth again
Scene 5 The Wedding Beano

NOTE: Act I, Scenes 2 and 4; Act II, Scenes 2 and 4 are either tabs or front cloth. Act I, Scenes 2 and 4; Act II, Scene 4 could all be the same if required. Act I, Scenes 1 and 3 could with adjustments be the same if this economy is of help

Description of Characters

Jack is a romantic dreamer, warm hearted so that he becomes emotional when having to sell Daisy the Cow, but also he is a brave hero. Preferably a female part.

The Princess must really struggle and fight and kick Fleshcreep, the Giant's Henchman so that the audience will cheer her on when she is defiant.

Dame Trot is the comedy Dame but is seriously emotional about selling the Cow and her famous scene of tragic dismay at finding the beans are not gold after all, should be played with great sincerity and she is enraged with her son Jack at this moment.

The King is daft, is comically scared ofthe Giant and he fancies Dame Trot.

The Giant, if in a medium or large auditorium, needs an offstage voice that can boom loudly and deeply into an offstage microphone. His is not a long part because he can outstay his welcome but if your cast includes a bass baritone (or someone that can almost be one) then the short "deep down ballad" he sings is a good idea. The Giant is the character that the audience is waiting for so he needs to be taken just that extra bit more seriously. Please see the costume notes about him and his height.

Fleshcreep is an immortal so he should perhaps have a green face. A highly sinister make-up and acting performance are needed as the entire cast is terrified of him and this fact must ring true. His villainy not only helps the story but also works as a butt for the comics. He is devious and horrible, yet the part should be played with relish.

Daisy the Cow. The audience will fall in love with Daisy and this makes the part very well worth playing for the (usually female) occupants of the cow costume. The head on one side or slowly lowered makes good mimed pathos and she can "moooo" whenever she thinks fit.

The Vegetable Fairy. The actress playing this rewarding part should not entirely rely on the comedy rhyming couplets too much, as Pantomime is a visual art so her props and comedy business are important. A mild rustic accent works well and it is best to play her with wild optimism and fun and never be "downbeat".

Silly Billy is a personality part with emphasis on comedy. Perhaps he looks a bit "country yokel" with battered hat and smock—if so his style must not clash with the Vegetable Fairy and must remain a personality part.

Clarence Clanger the Town Crier can be a fat red cheeked bluff man like the Beadle in Oliver Twist. Or he is an ex-sergeant major with a bristling moustache. Or, if played young, or by an actress, let the ringing of the bell drive the cast crazy when they hear it and let him or her have a cheeky almost cocky personality.

Spick and Span. Sergeant Spick and Corporal Span are a sort of military version of the traditional panto broker's men parts. It is traditional that they continually hit each other and fall down and are slapstick and the audience does like them played that way. But they can be played as Women's Army in which case they become a military version of the Ugly Sisters in style, though they need not be ugly, just a bit florid.

Mrs Blodwyn Blunderbore. Her make-up, voice and acting are menacing and splendidly melodramatic so that—like Fleshcreep—the cast are terrified of her and thus she works the comedy. She may wish to acquire a Welsh accent, in which case a bit of simple re-phrasing with a few "boyos" and "indeed-to-goodnesses" will help. The more horrible she is the better the comedy scenes work in Act II. She is not a panto witch, but she is played in the French Revolution Tricoteuse style.

The Dreaded Dragon is not dreaded at all when we meet it. Preferably played by an actress, the Dragon is cuddly and jigs about in its scene and song.

Costumes

Pantomime medieval is best for this subject though of course not essential.

The **Villagers, Townsfolk** (perhaps a couple of Gypsies in the cattle market scene) the Prisoners of the Giant (who are again the Villagers in rags), and Finale Scene are all straightforward costumes.

The **King** and **Princess** are richly dressed, the King comically so.

The **Dame** can have many costumes because this is pantomime tradition, though she could manage with almost one costume because of the story.

Jack and **Silly Billy** are village lads, Silly Billy comically so.

Clarence Clanger needs a three-cornered hat and a hand bell and perhaps a beadle-style costume.

Sergeant Spick and **Corporal Span** wear bright and gaudy guardsmen uniforms which should be a bit comical. If these two parts are played by actresses then the costumes can be a comedy version of drum majorettes with trousers.

Daisy the Cow is the same style of costume as a pantomime horse. The udder is usually made of wood and can swing about as much as you like and there must be room in the udder area to let the actress/actor playing the back legs hold out a hand with the milk bottle (see text).

The **Dragon** is preferably played in a complete head mask so that we do not show the human face and thus spoil the illusion. It is a small cuddly dragon.

Fleshcreep is helped if he is given a cloak to swirl about and his costume is sinister, in keeping with his character.

The **Vegetable Fairy** is sometimes dressed as a leek. But any green and eccentric costume will be fine. To dress her as a straightforward Fairy seems to be missing an opportunity for creating a "fun" costume, but she must be able to move her arms freely if the costume is involved and vegetable style.

In a medium or small-scale production the Villagers can easily wear the same costumes throughout, as the entire adventure story takes place in one day.

The **Beanstalkland** costumes can be green Beanstalk style cloak and hat or cap worn over the basic Villager costume.

The Giant's Costume

The most complicated and interesting costume problem is the Giant. If a Giant's costume is not going to be hired, here are some suggestions that may be of help.

To build up his height we need a straightforward pair of boots nailed on to very high sole and heel platforms made of wood. This can add a foot to his stature. If this pair of boots are awkward and clumsy that is in keeping with his character.

It will help further to achieve the necessary height effect by a big wig that the actor wears with some padding in it so that it really feels more like a hat to the actor. It may need elastic under the chin to hold it in place. The huge domed forehead comes down to a pair of bushy eyebrows—below this it is the actor's face (real), though with a big moustache and big beard. A very tall hat with feathers in it sticking upwards is also a help for height.

It may be possible to use an entire big head mask of the type that was called a "Big Head" in Victorian pantomime. It rests on the shoulders and the wearer looks through the mask's open mouth for vision.

It is possible—as his scene is not all that long—that the giant problem is solved by one actor sitting on the shoulders of another and his coat or smock hangs right down, almost to the floor; but this idea is tiring for the actor below.

The body bulk and sometimes the building up of the shoulders and head is usually done with foam rubber.

His arms must be practical and the gloves that are made to look like huge hands should allow for him to hold his big club and thus fight with Jack. (See text for fight details.)

Not only the costume but other things in this scene help to give the illusion of a terrifying Giant. Dim lighting and probably someone roaring and speaking the lines *close to* the offstage microphone to ensure a thunderous deep voice. When the dual is fought, *Jack* needs much agility as he jumps about, convincing the audience that he is fighting a duel with the Giant who is, in fact, going to have to be fairly stationary. Loud dramatic music, lightning flashes or Strobe lighting—all these things help the duel to be a good moment of theatre and prevent the Giant Scene from being an anticlimax.

The Giant's death is most effective if there is a great dying roar at the offstage microphone, a dramatic chord, and the Giant lurches forward over the table and is then still. He should on no account fall to the floor as this is dangerous because of the costume.

Scenery Note

The Village is with cottages and trees, but any trick props for the Fairy's "magic that goes wrong" is best if it is thought about right from the first scenery discussion. (See text for suggested Fairy props.)

The Cattle Fair should have some flags and bunting so that the "mind reading" routine seems to belong in this fairground cattle market scene. It is possible for it to be Scene 1 "tarted up" with flags etc. but of course it is best as a Pantomime Mediaeval Town. UC is the Magic Sword in the Magic Stone—please see text.

The Cottage Interior is entirely subservient to how the beanstalk is made to seem to grow by magic. There is no need for any practical cottage scenery, such as shelves, all that is needed is an upstage cut-out shaped like a cottage interior with pointed roof, but the window must be practical in as much as it is already open so that the Dame can instantly throw the beans out in her fit of fury.

The Growth of the Beanstalk

The Fairy conjures up the Transformation, and the easiest way is U.-V. light. Stage assistants in black can remove the interior of the cottage plus furniture, which appears to dance in the air. Or the cottage is split and pulled off to each side, and we now see the groundrow of grass and weeds, etc. The stage is dark so we cannot see the wire but, as this wire is pulled upwards, so the U.-V. beanstalk starts to rise magically from behind the groundrow.

There can only be so much beanstalk unrolling, so soon other scenery must mask this moving beanstalk. As we are now in a magic place, "silver slash" could be used for this masking but best is a backcloth designed as though a vast network of beanstalks. The beanstalk *can* stop rolling and this stationary beanstalk would be seen for the rest of the scene, and perhaps beanstalk-style wings can be moved on from the sides or flown in.

So we have gone from the beanstalk growing on an empty blacked out stage to a stage that is "all beanstalk" and it is now Beanstalkland in the sunshine. If U.-V. light is not possible, then the window can be made in the upstage cottage cut out an exaggerated size—say six foot wide by four foot in height—so that the audience can very clearly see through it, at the garden backing or just a plain light blue cyclorama.

This window has a central "post" to it, dividing the window, just as one sees in many windows. Behind this central post is the hidden nylon wire or rope. Pull the wire or rope, and soon the beanstalk (which must of course be wider than this central post of the window) appears and is seen to be growing outside the window.

What we don't want—and what you may have seen even in lavish professional pantomimes—is a rope or nylon wire showing clearly so that the whole audience knows perfectly well that the rope is to soon cause the beanstalk to grow. This is the story's famous moment and if possible, we do want the beanstalk to grow magically. You may find that after the beanstalk has grown you need to draw tabs or have a Beanstalk style frontcloth and in front of this Magic People sing or dance or both. But usually this isn't necessary.

A rope ladder or a wooden ladder disguised as a beanstalk is tempting but the best way is to turn the whole scene into Beanstalkland and not have Jack climbing. It is true that this is a famous moment, but it can be dangerous. Jack will not want to climb very high so it can be an anti-climax. Also, it is tricky to pull a heavy rope ladder, disguised as the beanstalk, upwards from the groundrow.

The other scenes in both acts are clearly explained in the script and are simple.

Production Notes

Music. There are, deliberately, few solos. If one of the cast has an excellent voice, then the music suggestions can easily be adapted to suit this fact. See **Musical Numbers.**

Snow effects. These can be made either by a lighting effect or by a cloud of torn pieces of paper thrown from the wings by a stage-hand standing on a ladder—the Fairy being near the wings for this moment.

Scene change to the **Cattle Market.** The previous frontcloth scene should be enough to cover the change, but if the set is an elaborate one, requiring more time, then Jack and the Dame, just before Jack's couplet and exit with Daisy, can sing a short sentimental love song about Daisy (with Daisy standing between them), and the lights can be brought down to a spot on the three of them.

Act I, Scenes 4/5. If required, the Chorus can enter at the end of Scene 4 so that the song becomes a Production Number. During it, the tabs can open (or the frontcloth be flown) so that the Production Number ends in the cottage interior, which is a full stage set. It must be remembered that there is not much time before Singers and Dancers are needed in the Transformation Scene, so that in (yet another variation) just a few people join Jack and Billy. During this number, or during the Black-out, the log that Daisy sat on is removed.

"Baby and bath" sequence. It is important that the baby is quite clearly a doll and is treated as a doll. This is an updated 1815 Grimaldi comedy scene, and it is necessary to avoid the "sadism to the baby" that was a feature of Regency comedy.

Fight between Fleshcreep and the Dame. This pantomime fight idea has to have "audience recognition", and whatever is the current trend on television should supply that. If, however, this topical idea is impracticable, then the Fairy can announce "Supersonic Sarah", and the Dame can enter in some Outer Space military uniform.

The **Vegetable Fairy.** Sometimes the lighting effects accidentally do work for the Fairy, and she has then lost her audience laugh. It is a good idea for her to keep the following couplet in case of this emergency. If said as an *ad lib.*, it should receive applause:

What on earth has happened tonight
Some of my magic is *going right*!

Musical Numbers

Permission to perform this pantomime DOES NOT include permission to use copyright songs and music. Please read the notice supplied by the Performing Right Society very carefully.

The songs listed below are *only suggestions* for the type of music that can be used in this pantomime. Choice of music and songs is left to the discretion of the individual producer.

ACT I

Song 1	*On A Wonderful Day Like Today* A dance routine production number	Villagers and Princess
Song 2	*On The Sunny Side Of The Street* The Audience can join in this one, the Villagers perhaps entering, strolling in tempo, making an exit on the last note	Silly Billy
Song 3	*It's Not Where You Start It's Where You Finish* Song and dance production number	Jack and Villagers
	Charleston—Can-Can—Polka A dance competition between the Dame and the Cow. They dance about eight bars of the three up-tempo bouncy songs, such as the ones mentioned above	Dame, Silly Billy and Cow
Song 3(a)	Reprise of Song 3	Jack, Spick, Span, Clarence and Villagers
Song 4	*You're My Everything* One verse of this song is sung with great emotion	Jack, Dame, Cow
Song 5	*This Is The Simple Life*	Townsfolk (perhaps Gypsies, Clarence and Princess too)
Song 5(a)	*A Pretty Girl Is Like A Melody* Incidental music played gently under the scene	

Song 5(b)	*In A Persian Market Place* Incidental music played during "Mind-Reading" sequence. You may want to include the music for "Fry's Turkish Delight" as well!	
Song 6	*Money, Money, Money* A duet in which the Audience can join in by clapping	Jack and Billy
Song 7	*Old Macdonald Had A Farm* This is a crazy comedy quartet song with movement and business, the dafter the animal noises are the better	Dame, King, Spick and Span
Song 8	*Climb Every Mountain* For the short Transformation Scene Ballet the tempo needs to be made into a slow waltz. For the vocal sung by the Magic Beanstalk People it becomes a ballad. For the "Interval Curtain Moment" when Jack enters in his armour with a sword, he and the others reprise it for eight bars at a dramatic tempo	Beanstalk People

ACT II

Song 9	*Sing Hallelujah* They are the Giant's prisoners in torn clothes and they sing this number with strange spooky lighting—it is almost a voodoo style number. For the second chorus, let the middle with lyric about "Satan" be a nasty solo for Fleshcreep, then return to the song and dance OR *Rockin' All Over The World* The other way to open Act II is to have comically eccentric animals dancing a rock 'n' roll session. First there is serious and spooky music as they glide about, then suddenly they go into the rock number	The Villagers

Song 10	*White Christmas* Sung unaccompanied to cheer themselves up while the wicked Mrs Blunderbore enters for the joey-joey scene of "she's behind you!"	Dame, King, Silly Billy, Spick and Span
Song 11	*Puff The Magic Dragon* The terrifying Dragon turns out to be a nice cuddly one. The Audience may wish to clap and join in this number. Probably two choruses will be ample	Jack, the Dragon
Song 12	*Anything You Can Do I Can Do Better* They battle it out in this song. Like "Old Macdonald" it is comedy with business	Fairy and Fleshcreep
Song 13	*You Made Me Love You* Duet and dance, the song being stopped three times for "kiss it better" comedy business. Start the dancing fairly early as it is not just a sung duet	Dame and King
Song 14	*It's Love Makes The World Go Round* You may prefer a ballad from the Top Twenty here	Princess
Song 15	*Food, Glorious Food* A song and dance production number with the Villagers as Cooks using huge Giant-scale props. Mrs Blunderbore can be made the central person of this Production Number. If she sings she can parade about like a "Broadway Musical Comedy Star" or else she can conduct with a huge fork	Villagers
Song 16	Duet (short reprise)	Jack and Princess
Song 17	James Bond Theme This is played as loudly as possible while the Dame does her karate style comedy fight with Fleshcreep. The Dame being "Wonderwoman" or "Supersonic Sarah" (see production notes)	

Song 18	*Drinking* ("In Cellar Deep") This is a short parody of a Victorian ballad and its coda is very "baritone". It is sung at the offstage microphone by a bass baritone and it's chorus and comedy coda should be long enough to convey the Giant's personality to the Audience	Giant
Song 19	*Happiness* A triumphant song of victory in which the Audience can join	Company
Song 20	*Daisy Bell* (Daisy, Daisy)	Songsheet number
Song 21	Finale A reprise of an earlier song (perhaps No. 3)	Company

A licence issued by Samuel French Ltd to perform this play does NOT include permission to use any copyright music in the performance. The notice printed below on behalf of the Performing Right Society should be carefully read.
In case of difficulty in finding sheet music, FRANCIS MUSIC SUPPLY of Gerrard Strcet, London, W1, are usually most helpful.

The following statement concerning the use of music is printed here on behalf of the Performing Right Society Ltd, by whom it was supplied

The permission of the owner of the performing right in copyright music must be obtained before any public performance may be given, whether in conjunction with a play or sketch or otherwise, and this permission is just as necessary for amateur performances as for professional. The majority of copyright musical works (other than oratorios, musical plays and similar dramatico-musical works) are controlled in the British Commonwealth by the PERFORMING RIGHT SOCIETY LTD, 29–33 BERNERS STREET, LONDON W1P 4AA.

The Society's practice is to issue licences authorizing the use of its repertoire to the proprietors of premises at which music is publicly performed, or, alternatively, to the organizers of musical entertainments, but the Society does not require payment of fees by performers as such. Producers or promoters of plays, sketches, etc., at which music is to be performed, during or after the play or sketch, should ascertain whether the premises at which their performances are to be given are covered by a licence issued by the Society, and if they are not, should make application to the Society for particulars as to the fee payable.

ACT I

Prologue

This is played either in front of tabs that then open on to the Village Scene or else it is played in the Village Scene with no lighting upstage and the two Immortals are very much downstage in the lit area

There is a flash in the footlights. Fleshcreep the Giant's wicked Henchman, is already on stage, laughing demoniacally

Fleshcreep Ha ha ha ha ha!
Bats fly about and the moonbeams glisten
It's the midnight hour but LISTEN! LISTEN! (*He cups his hand to his ear melodramatically*)

We hear the Giant's voice booming

Giant (*on the offstage microphone*)
Fee fi fo fum
I smell the blood of an Englishman
Be he alive or be he dead
I'll grind his bones to make my bread.

Fleshcreep paces about

Fleshcreep Let darkness cover this land
Let everyone hear that roar
Yes hark to the dread command
of GIANT BLUNDERBORE!

He addresses the audience

You—(*local place*)—*fools*, how you cringe and quake!
The might of the Giant no-one shall break!
Ha ha ha . . .

His laugh is interrupted by a burst of fairy music

Vegetable Fairy enters R, *and optimistically waves her hand. Behind her back she hides a large prop leek*

Fairy Hullo, my dears! It's the middle of the night
But I'll make everything turn out right!
I'm the Vegetable Fairy!
I look after the plants and the flowers!

She turns to Fleshcreep

And although you *do* look scarey
I'll thwart you with my powers!

Fleshcreep How I hate the way you speak.
Your weakness I'll soon find

Fairy Never! Here is my magic leek
To make you lose your mind!

There is a flash. She produces her leek as though a magic wand and points it at him. Sarcastic and confident, he grabs hold of its end

Fleshcreep Huh! A vegetable is all you've got!
OW! The darned thing's boiling hot!

As he yells "OW" there is a further flash, he lets go of the leek, wrings his hand in pain—percussion noises. The Fairy laughs at him, he is enraged

In this battle we are going to fight
You'll end up in a mess.

Fairy Never! My friends will help me all right!
(*To the audience*) You'll help me won't you?

She conducts them with her leek and they shout

Audience *YES!*

With a loud dismissive snarl of "Huh" and waving his fist at the audience, Fleshcreep exits L. *The Fairy, waving her leek triumphantly, exits* R.

At the same time we see instant sunshine, or the tabs open and at once we are in—

Scene 1

THE VILLAGE OF PENNYFARTHING

A village with cottages and trees and open countryside at the back. By the Dame's cottage is a barrel or a large bucket from which the Fairy's flower will later grow by pulling upwards on a nylon wire. The Villagers are singing

SONG 1

During the song, the Princess enters, the singing Villagers bow and curtsey and the Princess joins them in the song and dance

After the song, Clarence Clanger the Town Crier, wearing a three-cornered hat enters, ringing a hand bell. All the Villagers pull faces and put their fingers in their ears

Clarence (*announcing to the audience importantly*) I am the Town Crier! My name is Clarence Clanger and I want to pronounce a pronouncement! If anyone kills Giant Blunderbore his reward will be the Princess's hand in marriage!

Princess Clarence, you announce that every day—(*to the Villagers*)—and it doesn't get us anywhere, does it?

Villagers No!

First Villager (*waving his fist in the air*) The Giant is a villain!
All (*chanting*) Death to the Giant! Death to the Giant!
Princess Yes, death to the Giant—but who's going to kill him?
Clarence (*shaking his head anxiously*) Your Highness, there isn't anyone!
Princess If only someone could come along and set us free! If only someone *could* kill the Giant!

Loud comedy fanfare

Second Villager That's the royal fanfare!
Princess That will be Father. Perhaps *he's* got some ideas!
Third Villager It's the King!
Fourth Villager It's His Royal Magnificence!
Clarence (*removing his hat with a flourish*) His Majesty, King Satupon the Seventh!

All bow and curtsy

Sergeant Spick and Corporal Span, in comedy Guards uniforms, enter carrying a sedan chair. It is a simple cutout held in front of the walking monarch. The King waves graciously from the chair, calling out "Hullo, hullo."

King (*to the audience*) Greetings, objects! (*To Spick and Span*) Lower the litter the quicker the better.
Spick } Pardon? { (*Speaking*
Span } { *together*)
King Lower the quicker the better the litter. (*He corrects himself*) Quicker the litter the better the—oh forget it!

He steps out or gets off the chair while Guardsmen Spick and Span smartly move forward away from the chair with plenty of complicated foot stamping and their comedy salute and stand at attention on each side of the King, with their hands held out, palm upwards

(*Seeing their hands*) What are you doing that for? It's stopped raining.

The Villagers laugh

Oh, I understand—you want *paying*, don't you?
Spick } Yes, Your Maj! { (*Speaking*
Span } { *together*)
King How much?
Spick Twenty pounds.
Span Ten each.
King (*scandalized, to the audience*) Twenty pounds from—(*local railway station*)—to this village? TWENTY POUNDS?
Spick Yes, Your Maj.
Span Including VAT.
King Oh well, VAT's all right, then. (*To Spick*) I suppose you've got a wife and kids to support. Here you are. (*He counts as he mimes putting the coins into Spick's hand*) One—two . . . How many kids have you got?

Spick Seven.

King (*counting more "money" into Spick's hand*) Eight, nine, ten. That's you paid. (*To Span*) Now, Corporal, you live near me don't you—what number is your house?

Span Number eight.

King Really? (*He counts into Span's hand*) Nine, ten. There you are! (*Cheerfully*) Good day, gentlemen!

Spick
Span } (*with bewildered looks*) Good day, Your Maj! { (*Speaking together*)

The Villagers laugh

Spick and Span exit with the sedan chair

King Remove the litter! Keep Britain Tidy! (*To the audience*) Well, folks, I must introduce myself. I am King Satupon the Seventh! (*Dramatically and patriotically*) Yes, I am your *KING!*

He reacts to the fact that the audience has not responded to this

When you see the King all you ladies should curtsy and all you gentlemen should bow! (*He admits defeat*) Oh all right, you can wave instead. (*He waves to various sections of the audience*) Greetings! Greetings! Happy New Year! (*Waving to the front row*) The front row! Where they only eat fish and chips out of the *Daily Telegraph*! (*Waving to another area*) Oh look, the Muppets! And look, there's a group not waving to me at all. Stuffy lot. Well, they come from—(*local snob area*)!

Princess Oh Father, how can you be so cheerful! What are we going to do about the Giant?

King (*to her and the Villagers*) Now don't worry, anyone, don't panic, because if we keep a stiff upper lip and—

Dramatic chord

Fleshcreep enters fast and stands by the King but unseen by him. He carries a whip

—stick out our chests and smile and say—

Fleshcreep Silence, fool!

King (*continuing*)—"Silence, fool". That's not right. (*He sees him*) AAAH! It's Evil Canevil—(*or some television villain or politician*)!

Fleshcreep You know quite well who I am. (*To the Villagers*) And so do you. (*He walks along the footlights addressing the audience*) So do you, you crummy collection of—(*local place*)—nitwits! (*As though audience has reacted, as they may well have done*) And don't you dare answer me back like that or I'll come down there and have a quick whip-round! (*He cracks his whip*) My name is *Fleshcreep*, the Giant's Henchman, and he's looking for humans like you—Mums, Dads and Kiddy Widdies! He's not so fond of the Dads, they're a bit tough and they stick in his gullet, but he likes a NICE, PLUMP, JUICY Mum for supper and for breakfast he just *loves* little boys and girls. (*Cracking his whip*) Ha ha ha!

To everyone on stage

He wants villagers for his slaves!
And money, far far more!
And Kiddy Widdies for breakfast!
He is GIANT BLUNDERBORE!
Ha ha ha!

With a final crack of his whip Fleshcreep exits

The Princess runs sobbing to the King

Princess Oh, Father!
King It's all right, dear. We must rally everyone! (*To Clarence*) Call for Silly Billy!
Clarence (*shouting*) Silly Billy! Calling Silly Billy! (*He rings his bell*)
First Villager He'll cheer us up!

All laugh and agree and start to exit

All (*calling*) Silly Billy—where are you Silly Billy?

All exit looking for Silly Billy

One Girl remains. We hear a frightening thud—thud—thud sound

Girl (*terrified*) Giant Blunderbore!

The thud—thuds continue, because now Silly Billy enters beating a drum, and this is the thud—thud noise we can hear

(*Indignantly*) Billy!
Billy (*laughing, as he hands her the drum and stick*) Are you angry?
Girl I'm not angry, I'm *furious!*

The Girl storms off, taking the drum with her

Billy (*to the audience*) Sorry about that. (*He calls happily*) Hullo kids—I'm Silly Billy! I'm Jack's brother! And me mum is Mrs Trot! And we've got a cow called Daisy! (*He calls again*) HULLO, KIDS! (*He reacts to the few replies*) Here, you're supposed to shout back! I know my *name* is Silly Billy but I'm not silly, am I?
Audience Yes!
Billy (*pointing to an imaginary person and laughing*) You—cheeky—did you say "Yes"? (*The audience shouts back*) Well, you're all in good voice so once more—hullo, kids!
Audience Hullo, Billy!
Billy Beautiful! Smashing! Makes me feel great and I can forget the Giant for a minute! (*He takes a bit of paper out of his pocket*) I've written a poem about the Giant so I'll read it to you. (*He reads out*) "Rowick eet roof troom teeg boony booma geeer." That's not right. Oh—sorry. (*He turns the bit of paper upside down*) I'll start again. (*He coughs importantly and then recites*) "The Giant". A poem.
He's as noisy as noisy can be.
Well he's got indigestion you see.

When he let out a burp
I felt such a twerp
'Cos everyone thought it was me!
Boom! Boom!

(*Laughing*) Oh I feel much better now! In fact, I feel like singing a song, so I will! Yes, I'm going to open my mouth and really throw myself into it! (*Music starts*) And you clap in time! That's it! Well, we've got to see the sunny side if we can! (*He sings*)

SONG 2

Perhaps some of the Villagers enter and join him and then exit on the last note

If alone, he sings the song walking to and fro across the stage, doing a definite turn at the side of the stage at the end of each eight bars, in American vaudeville style, and he keeps the tempo "bouncy"

Billy (*after the song*) That was great! (*Exiting*) I'm off now but I'll be back! HULLO, KIDS!
Audience Hullo, Billy!
Billy (*waving*) Ta ta!

Billy exits L *as there is a burst of fairy music and the Fairy enters* R. *She is a bit out of breath. The Lights dim, as she speaks*

Fairy Oh! I've come as quick as I may
And I'm in a bit of a hurry
I'm out of breath but I'm here to say
My dears, you mustn't worry!

I know *all* about the Giant
And of course we must be wary!
But as you see from my curious clothes
I'm the Vegetable Fairy!

Now I must *prove* I'm a Fairy
I'm never one to be lazy
So here we go! Watch this show!
Abracadabra! UPSADAISY!

She waves her wand or her "Leek wand" in one direction. At some completely different place, to percussion, a big daisy rises up, on a nylon wire, from a bucket or barrel

Where's the daisy? Nothing's happened! My magic's gone wrong again.
Audience Over there! Behind you!
Fairy Where? (*Some audience participation*) Oh, *there!* Thank you! Some better magic now! Watch this! (*She recites, waving her wand*)
Abracadabra Abracadee
Bring the sunshine up for me! *The Sunshine!*

Black-out, then Lights up again

I'll try again! (*She again waves her wand and recites*)
Cabbages, cauliflowers, carrots and peas,
Make the sun shine for me *please!*

Snow effects

Oh blimey. (*She shrugs*) If at first you don't succeed, give up! But *no*. I never give up. Not by a long lettuce! (*She laughs at her little joke and jigs about*)

Fleshcreep enters to dramatic chords

Fleshcreep Fairy, don't trample on my domains!
Fairy As if I would—they smell of drains!
Fleshcreep (*laughing dismissively*) Ha ha ha ha ha!
Fairy No need to laugh—instead take heed
A CHAMPION is what I need
Someone who'll fight my battle for me
Who'll kill the Giant and set us free!
Fleshcreep Your hero might be cheered by the crowds
But how is he going *to get up to the clouds?*

Pointing upwards as he deals this trump card, Fleshcreep exits laughing derisively

Fairy Now don't despair—have no fear
Something tells me my Champion's near!
The boy who is brave and courageous. What's more
The boy who will kill Giant Blunderbore!

She waves her wand, ushering on the Villagers and ushering in the up-tempo music

The Villagers enter as the Fairy exits optimistically

First Villager Have you heard the latest?
All No, what's that?
First Villager Jack's finished that contraption he's been working on!
Second Villager You mean the catapult to kill the Giant?

All laugh

First Villager Quiet, everyone—here's Jack now!

Jack enters, waving to the Villagers and then to the audience

Jack I'm Jack—and I'm all right! Yes, somehow, I'm going to make my way in the world! (*He sings*)

SONG 3

Wonderful day like Today

The song becomes a production number for Jack and the Villagers

(*After the number, to the audience*) Hullo everyone! I'm Jack Trot, and my mum and Billy and Daisy the Cow and me, we all live in the cottage over there. (*He points to it*)

The First Villager hands him large book, laughing as he does so, and sending Jack up

First Villager Here's the book from the village library.
Jack (*taking it and looking through it eagerly*) Thanks! Fabulous! That's what you call a *big* adventure story!
Second Villager What's the book, Jack?
Jack This one's about Sir Lancelot—he was a brave knight, always dressed in shining armour!
Third Villager What, *another* one?

The Villagers laugh

Jack Oh I never get tired of reading about knights in armour! I wish *I* could do something brave and heroic! That's why I asked you to help me build the great catapult, to kill Giant Blunderbore! Have a look, see how we're getting on!

The big medieval-looking catapult is pushed onstage on a trolley, a converted supermarket trolley, or one of the Villagers staggers on with a big four foot high "Y" shaped catapult with a band of black cloth representing elastic, and another Villager holds a football painted black as the catapult pellet

There—What d'you think of it so far?
Villagers Rubbish!
Jack (*laughing*) I thought you'd say that, but believe me it *will* work!

The Villagers laugh and ridicule the catapult, which is held up, pointing to it

No, listen to me! You know how the Giant comes clumping through the village every afternoon?
Villagers Yes!
Jack Well next time he comes by, is he in for a surprise! (*To the two Villagers*) That's it—You hold up the catapult, you put the stone in the sling, you fire the catapult—SPLAT! No more Giant, no more taxes, we'll be free!
Villagers Hurray!
Jack I must tell my mum about the catapult! I tell my mum everything! I wonder where she is? Probably in—(*local coffee bar or hotel*)! Mum! Where are you?
Villagers Mrs Trot! Dame Trot! Where are you? Dame Trot!

All exit, calling for Dame Trot

Vaudeville music

The Dame enters from a different place

Dame Hullo, people! I'm Dame Trot, but you can call me Trotty! Come on then, call out Trotty! (*She conducts them as they shout*) And again!

Audience Trotty!
Dame (*to an imaginary person*) No, dear, *Trotty*, not potty. (*She points to another imaginary person*) And you, you over there, you said Botty. Oh yes he did!
Audience Oh no he didn't!
Dame Oh yes he *did!*
Audience Oh no he didn't!
Dame Did—did—did!
Audience Didn't—didn't—didn't!
Dame (*loudly*) Oh no he didn't *did!* (*She laughs*) There, that got you! But I don't know why I'm messing about like this when it's time I was milking the cow. (*She looks round*) Where is Daisy? (*She calls*) Daisy!

Billy enters, the Dame looks offstage

Billy Hullo, kids!
Audience Hullo, Billy!
Billy Hullo, Mother! What are you looking for?
Dame Daisy. It's milking time.
Billy I'll help you find her. (*Calls*) Daisy!
Dame (*calling*) Daisy! She can't hear us. (*To the audience*) Will you call for Daisy the Cow?
Audience Yes!

All call for Daisy

Daisy enters to the music of "*Daisy, Daisy, give me your answer do*"

Dame Bow to the ladies and gentlemen and boys and girls.

Daisy does, then she turns sideways and the Dame points to the udder and the tail which Billy lifts up to show it off to the audience

Isn't she lovely? She's got four hanger-downers and a swisher. (*To the Cow*) Well, dear, it's milking time and you like to be milked don't you?

The Cow shakes her head

Of course you do!
Billy Some cows don't. (*He recites*)
I knew a girl whose name was Deena
She milked a cow with a vacuum cleaner
Along came the farmer and gave her the sack
So she turned the cow over and poured it all back!
Dame (*to the Cow*) Yes, it's good isn't it? (*To the Audience*) It's by Kipling. He also makes exceedingly good cakes.
Daisy Moooo!
Billy (*holding up the end of the tail and sternly speaking "into" it as though it is a speaking tube*) Daisy—Listen—we want some milk. Now stand there like a good girl and I'll nip off and get the bucket.

Billy exits

Dame And I'll get the stool.

The Dame goes up stage and collects the stool. Daisy frisks and deliberately moves to another place on the stage

Billy enters with a bucket

Billy (*returning*) That's it—where's she gone? What are you doing up there? Honest, you are a silly cow.
Dame *What?*
Billy Not you, Mum!

The Dame places the bucket and stool, bending over to do so. The Cow comes up and kicks her bottom, then frisks about again

Dame OW! Stop it, Daisy! You're behaving like two men in a skin.

Billy takes the bucket and puts it firmly on the ground

Billy *There.*

The Cow walks to it, pauses, then walks on

Oh you're beyond the pail!
Dame Come on, Daisy, milking time. I'm sitting down waiting.

The Dame sits on the stool, pats her lap as though straightening her apron. The Cow backs and its rear half sits on the Dame's lap. The Dame yells

I'm sitting down, not you!

Both get up. The Cow sways the udder

Look, Billy—bagpipes!
Billy (*watching the Cow swaying*) She's going to make a milk-shake!
Dame Let's milk her the new way. (*She quickly writes on a bit of paper from her apron, "One pint today please" speaking the words as she does*)

The Dame puts the note in the Cow's mouth. She pauses—drum roll—then she leans down and collects a full bottle of milk from the udder area—we can clearly see the person's hand holding it out—there is a cymbal crash as though at the end of a trick, and the audience applauds

In one end and out the udder!

Billy uses the Cow's tail as a pump. A tin falls on the ground from the udder area. He picks it up, rattles it, listens

Billy There's nothing in it. Oh, of course, it's evaporated.
Dame Let me think—what else comes out of cows?
Billy What comes out of cows? (*He repeats*) What comes out of cows?
Dame (*collecting a toy paddle-boat from out of the udder area and holding it up*) The Isle of Wight Ferry!

Laughing, the Cow jumps up and down and then collapses on the ground

(*Trying to help the Cow*) Come, Daisy, upsadaisy! (*She struggles to lift the rear half up*)
Billy Don't worry, Mum, I'll cantilever her up.

He gets under Cow and pushes her back up so that Daisy is standing up correctly

Dame Well you can't—a—lever—down there!

The Cow collapses completely on to Billy, who is flat on the floor

You look like President Cow Under! (*To Daisy*) Daisy, you're leading us a merry dance!

At this the Cow moves clear of Billy, and Billy gets up

Oh of course! She wants to dance, don't you?

The Cow nods

Well, I'm a marvellous dancer, so she won't be as good as me, will she, boys and girls?

Audience Yes!

Dame (*with more comedy conceit*) *Yes?* Of course she won't. Look at this!

Music. The Dame dances something such as a quick Charleston bit, Billy claps in time, then the Dame turns to the Cow

Your turn, Daisy.

The Cow dances. Billy claps in time, the Dame scoffs at the Cow's dance

Billy (*to the audience*) Which was better?

Audience *Daisy!*

Dame (*offended*) What? *Daisy?*

Audience Yes!

The Dame is taken aback

Dame But *I'm* the best dancer, oh yes I am!

Billy (*conducting the audience*) Oh no you're not! Try it again, Mum—(*to the audience*)—and Daisy will win again, won't she?

Audience Yes!

The Dame does another very quick dance, maybe the Can-Can, and then the Cow dances its quick dance to the music

Billy Which was better?

Audience Daisy!

Dame Oh no, she's not!

Audience (*conducted by Billy*) Oh yes, she is!

Dame Well *I'll* win the third time. Here, Billy, you and me will do a polka—that'll fool her.

To polka music Billy and the Dame do a few steps, then watch Daisy. The two people inside the Cow skin stand upright, and turn inwards as though a hinge is halfway along Daisy's body, and dance the polka, now looking like a camel. Billy and the Dame laugh, applaud Daisy as well as the audience

Billy She's the best, Mum!

Dame Well perhaps she *is* the best. After all, she's got four legs and I've got only two!

All three exit, to a few bars of loud vaudeville music. Sinister music as Fleshcreep enters where the catapult is now off or at the wings

Fleshcreep (*laughing and pointing off to it*) A catapult! Ha ha ha ha! (*He recites*)

So Jack thinks he'll hit the Giant!
Just let the silly boy try!
He's forgotten that I am Fleshcreep—
Giant Blunderbore's spy!
He thinks he'll hit the Giant's head
And knock the Giant to the floor
But my master will by-pass the village instead
'Cos I'll *tell* Giant Blunderbore!

He starts to exit

(*To the audience*) All you humans are *so stupid!*

Fleshcreep exits L, *and Jack enters* R, *with the book tucked in his belt. The Princess enters, elsewhere*

Jack Princess!
Princess Jack! I've been looking for you. (*She laughs*) And you've got another book of adventures!
Jack Yes—I may not be rich but no one can say I'm not a dreamer!
Princess If only you *were* rich, then my father would let us marry.
Jack Well, I'm not. I haven't a bean.
Princess "I haven't a *bean*?"—what a funny phrase!
Jack I read it in a book somewhere. (*He takes out book excitedly*) This one is about Sir Lancelot!
Princess And last week you had one about Robin Hood! Oh Jack, you're not very practical, are you?
Jack Of course I am! If I had a bow and arrow like Robin Hood, I'd fire it at the Giant and kill him! Pow! (*He makes out he's firing an arrow at the sky*)
Princess The arrow would have to go rather a long way, wouldn't it? He lives up in Cloudland!
Jack Oh you're right—I'm hopeless . . .
Princess No you're not, you're romantic. That's why I love you.

It used to be traditional to have a duet here. This is an optional "extra" as it slows the pace in Act I

They hold hands but at once we hear the Giant roaring on the offstage microphone and the stage darkens immediately

Giant (*off*)

Feee fi fo fum
I smell the blood of an Englishman!

Jack and the Princess are scared

The King, Clarence, Sergeant Spick and Corporal Span, who give the audience their comedy salute, the two Villagers, who are again holding the catapult and ball, and the other Villagers all enter in a great panic, looking upwards as though to see the approaching Giant. Some are pointing upwards

King (*advancing forward cheerfully to Jack*) Hullo! Hullo! Hullo! (*He realizes, and stops dead*) IT'S THE GIANT! (*He walks backward, retreating from Jack*) Good-bye! Good-bye! Good-bye!
Princess Where are you going?
King Home!
Spick
Span } No you're not! { (*Speaking together*)

The King tries to exit backwards between Spick and Span, who hook their arms into his and thus lift him up and bring him back C, *he struggling and doing a bicycle-pedalling movement with his legs*

King Hey! Put me down! I'm a King!
Jack Come on, everybody, stand by!

The roars become continuous and we hear the thud—thud—thud of the Giant's steps. All look upwards to the down L *corner of the stage and group hopefully around the two Villagers and the catapult*

Giant (*off*) Ha ha ha ha ha!

The Giant's laughter starts to fade, so does the thud—thud of his footsteps

Jack (*dismayed*) He's going the other way! That means we can't hit him!
Princess He's never gone the other way before! He always walks through the village so he can frighten us!
Jack Someone must have told him about the catapult. (*To the Villagers*) I bet it was that horrible Henchman!
All Yes! The Henchman! The Henchman!

General consternation. Clarence shakes violently

King Clarence, what's the matter?
Clarence Ker—ker—ker—ker—Clarence has got the ker—ker—ker—collywobbles! I always get them when the Giant's about.
Princess Oh Jack, what are we going to do?
Jack (*with a sudden inspiration*) Tell you what—*I'll* fight the Giant!

At this, the crowd laugh and whistle, so he turns to the Princess

Princess, *you* think I can do it, don't you?
Princess Of course I do! (*She appeals to the others*)
All Hooray!

Jack sings a reprise of his song

Wonderful day

SONG 3A

This is a short Production Number for all on stage. As it ends, Black-out

Scene 2

OUTSIDE DAISY'S COWSHED IN THE VILLAGE

Tabs or a front cloth

The Dame enters

Dame Oh dear, oh dear. We've got no money, we can't pay the rent, I don't know what we're going to do . . .

Fleshcreep enters

Fleshcreep Psssst! Pssssst!
Dame Someone's left the gas on. (*She now sees Fleshcreep*) Oh, it's Wurzel Gummidge!
Fleshcreep Everyone in the village has paid the Giant's Tax except you. *What about the taxes?*
Dame I don't use taxis—only buses.
Fleshcreep *I* am the Giant's Henchman!
Dame *Je suis, tu es, il est, nous sommes . . .*
Fleshcreep (*furiously*) I said Henchman not Frenchman! Unless you pay the tax you'll be kicked out of your cottage.
Dame You mean—(*clutching her chest dramatically*)—I'll have no roof to my mouth?
Fleshcreep You can't even pay the rent!
Dame I know that.
Fleshcreep And what about the rates?
Dame (*in a refined voice*) We don't have rates, only "mayce".
Fleshcreep (*loudly*) I warn you again. Unless you pay the Giant's Tax by midday tomorrow, I'll have you thrown out on your ear, you stupid old woman. I am all powerful, there is nothing I can't do! *Do you hear me?*
Dame Yes, Brian Clough.
Fleshcreep Bah!

Fleshcreep exits

Dame What am I going to *do?* What am I going to *do?*

Jack enters anxiously, leading Daisy the Cow

Jack Mum, are you all right? That was the Giant's Henchman, wasn't it? What did he want?
Dame Oh Jack, we've got to get some money or we'll be flung out of our home!
Jack We'll have to sell something, but what?

Music plays softly and sentimentally under the following

Oh Mum, there's only one thing we can sell. (*In a loud whisper to her as an aside*) We'll have to sell D-A-I-Z-E-E.
Dame (*shattered*) Jack! Sell the K-O-W?
Jack (*unhappy about it*) Well, it's the cattle market in the town this after-

noon. I *could* take her along. (*He realizes what he has said*) Oh no, I can't, I can't—poor Daisy . . . (*He pats the Cow*)

Dame Oh dear, this is very difficult . . .

Jack It's all right, Mum, leave it to me. (*With false cheerfulness*) Daisy, you've heard of the wicked Giant!

Daisy jumps and frisks about

Now don't be silly, he isn't here!

Dame But he *might* come so we want to send you to somewhere safe.

Jack So—(*he gulps*)—I'm going to take you to the cattle market.

Dame Yes. Jack's going to sell you to some nice kind gentleman who loves Cows! Now you'll enjoy that won't you?

Daisy shakes her head

Dame
Jack } Aaaaaah . . . { (*Speaking together*)

The audience join in

Dame Oh you *will*, Daisy! And when somebody gets brave enough to kill the Giant, we'll fetch you home again!

Jack (*emotionally*) Poor old thing. She's all we've got left. I'll find you a nice home, I'm sure I will. Now say good-bye to everyone, like a good girl.

Jack takes Daisy's rope halter and the Cow bows to the audience

Although it almost breaks my heart
Even the best of freiends must part.

Jack exits with Daisy. The Dame bursts into loud sobs, then even louder sobs, then declaims loudly and tragically

Dame Poor Daisy's gone to meet her doom
It's left an ache in my bozoom!

Dramatic chord. Black-out

OPTIONAL SONG 4 (*see music details at beginning of script*)

Scene 3

THE CATTLE MARKET IN THE NEARBY TOWN

This could be the same as Scene 1, *with flags and bunting everywhere and a large sign, pointing off, in clumsy letters saying "TO CATTLE MARKET". If a new scene is possible, this is a pantomime medieval town decked out with flags and flower garlands and bunting, for this Cattle Market Day. Perhaps fruit and vegetable stalls*

Prominent in the scene, up C, *under some sort of roof or wooden/ironwork canopy there is a big block of stone about three foot square. In it, thrust in at an angle, is a ceremonial sword*

The Princess, Clarence and the Townsfolk are assembled and perhaps there are a couple of Gypsy Girls among them selling bunches of flowers

Clarence (*ringing his bell, then announcing*) Your Royal Highness and everyone else, it is Cattle Market Day!

All cheer and sing and dance

SONG 5

After the song and dance, Clarence rings his bell again

(*Announcing*) Has everyone present tried to pull the sword out of the stone?

He points to the sword, and all look at it

All Yes!
First Townsman (*stepping forward*) I haven't!
Second Townsman Nor me!
Princess (*to the First Townsman*) They say it's King Arthur's Sword and it was put there by Merlin the Magician many years ago!
Clarence (*to the Second Townsman*) Whoever pulls the sword out of the stone will kill the Giant!
All (*nodding agreement*) That's right! That's the legend!
Princess (*to the two men who are now at the stone*) That's the ancient prophesy. (*To everyone*) And we're longing for it to be fulfilled, aren't we?
All Yes, Your Highness!

The First Townsman tries to pull the sword from the stone but cannot. All on stage sympathize

Second Man Let me have a try.

The Second Townsman mimes that he is desperately tugging at the sword. He has pushed up his sleeves and he pants hard as he tugs at the sword. But the sword remains intact. He shrugs, all sympathize

All It's a shame. I'm sorry. What a pity.
Princess (*to them both*) It needs great strength and they say it needs magic as well. Thank you for trying so hard.

Both men salute and wave to her, thanking her. Clarence rings his bell again

Clarence (*announcing*) His Magnificent Majesty King Satupon!

A comedy fanfare, the King enters followed by his two Guardsmen, Spick and Span

King (*as they enter*) Go away! GO AWAY!
Spick We want our money!
Span You owe us our wages!
King This is very embarrassing. (*To everyone*) I've got to sort out some business matters, so would you leave us?

All Yes, Your Majesty.

Everybody starts to exit

The Princess talks to the King

Princess Is somebody worrying you, Father?
King Yes dear. He's horrible, hideous, cruel and wicked.
Princess You mean Giant Blunderbore?
King No, Sir Geoffrey Howe—(*or whoever is Chancellor of the Exchequer*)
Princess (*laughing*) Then I'll leave you to it.

The Princess exits after the Townsfolk

Spick Come on Mr King, pay us our wages!
Span Yes pay up, like you said you would!
King I can't pay up! I haven't any money—I've just paid the palace staff.
Spick How much was that?
King Well I've got thirteen people working at the palace and they earn seven pounds each. (*Depressed*) That's ninety-one pounds a week I have to pay out.
Span No it's not, it's twenty-eight pounds a week!
King Twenty-eight pounds? Thirteen people earning seven pounds a week —thirteen times seven is ninety-one, so that's ninety-one pounds!
Spick Of course it isn't, it's twenty-eight pounds! Watch while we show you.
Span By an incredible stroke of luck there happens to be a blackboard and easel over there!

He points off, or the blackboard is by a market stall. Either Spick or Span bring the blackboard and chalk to the King C, *and while they do this the King remonstrates*

King (*to the audience*) They're trying to make out I've still got some money to pay them with. Well I haven't. (*Loudly*) Because thirteen times seven is ninety-one! Everyone knows that!
Spick Right, here we go. Thirteen times seven is twenty-eight—

Span chalks the numbers on the blackboard as Spick talks

—three times seven is twenty-one, one times seven is seven, seven plus twenty-one is twenty-eight.

Span chalks up this sum, starting with the "'7' at the top of the blackboard

```
 7
13
—
21
 7
—
28
```

King That can't be right! You've tricked me somewhere! (*He is puzzled*)

Spick Tricked you? Of course I haven't tricked you! Corporal write out thirteen seven times.
Span Right, Sarge.

Spick quickly writes on the blackboard

13
13
13
13
13
13
13
—

Spick And now to prove I'm not cheating, we'll get *everybody* to do it for you. (*To the audience*) Let's add up the threes!

Spick points to the "3" *column and his finger moves upwards and the audience calls out* "*3-6-9-12-15-18-21*" *and then he points to the* "1" *at the top of the left hand column and calls out* "*22*". *Then travelling down the column he calls out with the audience* "*22-23-24-25-26-27-28*". *Span laughs, applauds Spick and gets the audience to applaud also*

Span (*to the King*) There you are! You only paid out twenty-eight pounds, so you've got plenty of money to pay us our wages!
King (*gazing at the blackboard*) What you've done is right—
Spick / **Span** Yes! (*Speaking together*)
King —but it's *wrong!* (*He shakes his head, confused*)
Spick It isn't wrong, it's right!
Span And it's right that you pay us our wages for the whole of last year because you haven't paid us a penny so far!
King (*incredulously*) Pay you two your wages for the whole of last year?
Spick / **Span** Yes! (*Speaking together*)
King But you didn't do *any* work last year!
Span What d'you mean, we didn't do any work last year?
King (*his turn to triumph now*) I'll show you. (*He collects the chalk*) You didn't do any work last year and I'll prove it. How many days in a year?
Spick / **Span** Three hundred and sixty-five. (*Speaking together*)
King Assuming it's a leap year?
Spick / **Span** (*pleased at this*) Three hundred and sixty-six! (*Speaking together*)

The King writes on the blackboard "*366*"

King How many hours do you work a day?
Spick / **Span** Eight hours. (*Speaking together*)

King Well that's a third of a day—that makes it two hundred and twenty-two. (*He writes this amount on the board*)

Spick
Span } Now wait a minute! { (*Speaking together*)

King You don't work Sundays do you?

Spick
Span } No. { (*Speaking together*)

King There are fifty-two Sundays in the year. That makes it seventy. (*He writes this amount on the board*)

Spick
Span } Now wait a minute! { (*Speaking together*)

King And you don't work Saturdays either, do you?

Spick
Span } No. { (*Speaking together*)

King Fifty-two Saturdays—that makes it eighteen. (*He writes the amount on the board*)

Spick
Span } Now wait a minute! { (*Speaking together*)

King How many Bank Holidays in the year?

Spick
Span } Four { (*Speaking together*)

King Then that makes it fourteen. (*He writes this down*)

Spick
Span } Now wait a minute! { (*Speaking together*)

King (*preparing for the kill*) Now, lads, did you have a holiday last year?

Spick
Span } Yes. { (*Speaking together*)

King How long was it?

Spick
Span } Two weeks. { (*Speaking together*)

King Two weeks? (*He triumphantly chalks "14" on the board and then "0"*) That's fourteen days, and fourteen from fourteen is nought. *So you didn't do any work last year!*

Spick (*confused*) I don't get it . . .

King (*in huge triumph*) No you don't! Good day!

Loud vaudeville music

The King exits followed by a confused Spick and Span who exit also, carrying the blackboard and easel. From the other side, Jack enters with Daisy the Cow. In one hand he holds her halter, in the other hand a bucket containing props

Jack Well here we are at the Cattle Market! So if we're going to sell you, we must make you look pretty, mustn't we, Daisy?

The Cow shakes her head

Now don't be silly, and stand still like a good girl.

Music plays some song connected with "Beauty" (5a) as Jack puts down the bucket and takes out the various props

Toothbrush!

He takes a two-foot-long "backbrush" from the bucket and quickly "cleans Daisy's teeth". If the cow can be made to show its teeth, Jack says "Oh it's Esther Rantzen!" (*or Ken Dodd, etc.*)

Lipstick!

He replaces the brush and takes out a two-foot-long lipstick and applies it to the cow's lips

Powder!

He replaces the lipstick and takes out a vast prop powder puff and dabs her nose, returns the puff to the bucket and takes out an attractive flat straw hat with a hole in it to put over her ear

And now, to look your best, your best Sunday hat!

He puts it on Daisy and ties the ribbon under her chin, feeling a bit emotional about her, then stands back

(*To the audience, very proudly*) Doesn't she look smashing? Give her a round of applause, come on!

Jack starts the applause, then collects a pencil and paper from the bucket

I must write out a list so that I remember all your selling points. Then I'll get a really good price for you. (*He starts writing*) One, milk yield eight pints. Two, you're ten years old. Three—oh drat, my pencil's bust and I haven't got a penknife. (*He casually looks round and sees the sword*) Oh, there's a sword! (*He goes to it, and casually and innocently pulls the ceremonial sword straight out of the stone*)

The Lights dim, just spotlight on Jack and the Cow—they both freeze into statues and there is a tingling musical effect

The Fairy enters R. *Fleshcreep enters* L. *They pose*

Fairy Fleshcreep, you villain, now I'm defiant!
At last I've a Champion to fight the Giant!

Fleshcreep So the magic sword made of magic steel
Has come out of the magic stone—big deal!

Fairy That's right, go on, laugh!
(*To the audience*) He thinks that I'm dumb.
But listen to me! WE SHALL OVERCOME!
This lad shall win through and the world
shall be free!

Fleshcreep Huh! I'll soon find a way to defeat him—
you'll see!

Fairy Never!
I'm the Vegetable Fairy, and I know my Onions!

She stands on tiptoe ready to exit in a fairylike way

And I'd exit on my points if it wasn't for
my bunions!

The Fairy and Fleshcreep exit R *and* L *respectively. Two of the Townsfolk enter*

Jack and the Cow return to normal life. Jack starts to sharpen the pencil with the sword and sees the two Townsfolk

Jack (*with great optimism*) Anybody want to buy a cow? She's a *good* cow, never loses her temper and kicks over the milk bucket! (*He puts down the sword on the stone but not back into it*)

The Townsfolk wonder about buying the Cow, but at once Daisy kicks over the bucket

The Townsfolk laugh, point rudely at the Cow and exit

Jack is aghast and worried because there has been no sale

Another couple of Townsfolk enter, a boy and girl gazing into each other's eyes romantically

Anybody want to buy a cow? She's a fine breed—she's a—(*local name*)—Angus! (*If possible, he uses an alliteration such as "she's an Aston Angus or a Falmouth Fresian, or whatever is a local "joke" place*)

The Romantic Couple continue across the stage, looking soppily at each other, and exit

Again Jack is worried

A Girl crosses the stage

Who wants to buy a Jersey?
Girl (*cheekily*) Who knitted it?

The Girl exits, leaving the anxious Jack. A third Couple enter and cross the stage

Jack Anybody want to buy a cow? She's very well behaved, never does anything she shouldn't!

The two Villagers admire Daisy, but she kicks the boy Villager on his seat. He lets out an indignant "OW" and exits with the equally indignant girl

Jack is desperate. The sentimental music that was played before is reprised. Jack collects the props and puts them in the bucket

(*As he does so, depressed and emotional*) No-one wants to buy you, old girl. I don't know what to do now. Mother will be ever so angry that I haven't been able to sell you. Oh Daisy, don't look at me like that! It makes me want to cry! Daisy, you're my best friend in all the world, you know that!

The Cow looks pathetic and Jack cries

Oh I *can't* sell you, Daisy. I can't—I just can't. Come on, old girl, let's go home. (*He calls out loudly*) *Home, Daisy, home!*

The music builds up loudly and emotionally as Jack and Daisy exit. From the other side, the Dame and Silly Billy enter to a few bars of comedy oriental music. They both wear comedy gypsy costumes or fezzes, and Billy carries a stool

Billy Hullo, kids!
Audience Hullo, Billy!
Billy (*to the Dame*) I feel so silly in this costume.
Dame You look lovely, dear, so shut up.
Billy But why have I got to dress up like this?
Dame Because we're going to do our mind reading act and if it's a success *we'll make some money!*
Billy With our mind-reading act?
Dame Certainly! This is the cattle fair! It's a perfect place to try it out! We'll have a practice run and then you see if we don't make some money.
Billy Shall I sit down now?
Dame Yes, you sit on the stool and I'll blindfold you.

Billy sits on the stool. The Dame takes a large piece of black transparent gauze and blindfolds him

I'll ask all our friends out there to help. (*To the audience*) You'll help won't you?
Audience Yes!
Dame (*to Billy*) Are you sitting comfortably?

Billy nods

Then we'll begin.
Billy It's Jackanory!
Dame (*running her hands over his head and chanting*) Aaaaah—aaaah . . . May the Power that comes out of the Earth now enter your brain.
Billy That's going to be difficult.
Dame Why?
Billy I haven't got one.

The Dame goes "all mysterious", and stupid-sounding oriental music (5b) is repeated quietly—over and over—for the routine which starts with her announcement to the audience

Dame Ladies and Gentlemen, I would like to prove to you that my partner has truly psychic powers!

She speaks to the now blindfolded Billy sitting on the stool

Let me test you right away—what am I thinking of now?
Billy Your next line of dialogue.

Dame (*laughing*) Absolutely correct! There, I've blindfolded you and now I'll go into the audience and test you out.

The Dame turns Billy round on the stool to confuse him then holds up her hands near his face

How many fingers have I got?

Billy Eleven.

Dame Nearly right! (*Covering up*) His powers are truly marvellous! He knows exactly what I am going to do. (*She starts to go into the audience*) I am going down—

Billy —the steps!

Dame Correct! And into—

Billy —the *audience!*

The Dame is now in the audience. The House Lights come up

Dame Correct! Amazing! Now the first object. (*She stands near a little boy*) I am going to take hold of a portion of this boy's head—so what have I got 'old of 'ere?

Billy His ear.

Dame Correct. Give him a big hand! (*Moving to a lady*) Now this lady has something on her finger. What is it?

Billy A nail.

Dame Nearly. I'll give you a clue. (*She imitates a telephone*) "Brrrrh, brrrrh".

Billy A lion, she's got a lion on her finger.

Dame No, if you don't get it right I'll *ring* your neck.

Billy A ring.

Dame Correct! Now this gentleman has something on his wrist. What is it?

Billy A wart.

Dame Now watch it—watch it. (*Pause*) You'll get it any second.

Billy A second-hand watch!

Dame Correct. And I have here a handkerchief with a lady's name on it—is it Bill or Freda?

Billy Bill.

Dame Nearly right. (*She holds up someone's pen*) And this object? Oh, you're bound to get this right—do you remember when we walked through that *sheep pen?*

Billy Sheep.

Dame Nearly.

Billy *Pen!* Ha ha—aren't I good?

Dame There's a lady over there with something on her head. What is it?

Billy A saucepan.

Dame It's blue.

Billy A blue saucepan.

Dame (*annoyed but covering up*) Very amusing—just what do you think you're *at?*

Billy "At"!

Dame (*bit fed up with him*) I should hope so too! And this lady here has just picked up something. What is it?
Billy Her husband.
Dame No, no, no, answer the question! *What is it?*
Billy (*thinking*) What is it—what is it . . .?
Dame (*getting impatient*) Yes, Silly Billy, what is it? (*Quickly returning to the stairs and on to the stage*) Oh you're no good at all! In fact, you're hopeless! I've been working myself stupid silly to get this act right and you don't care a fig! (*On the stage, angrily*) Oh what can I do with the boy. . . .

The House Lights fade

Clarence Clanger, or one of the Townsfolk—whoever is the more dignified —enters with a tray that has a string round his neck and attached to the front corners of the tray. On the tray are two or three cardboard plates with bright-coloured jelly on them or a brightly coloured "Instant Whip" mixture

Clarence (*calling*) Pies! Custard pies! Lovely custard pies! Custard pies!

The Dame reacts with wicked delight

Dame Aha!

She signals to Clarence and takes a cardboard plate from him. Clarence walks up to Billy and, curious, inspects him and laughs at him. So it is Clarence one side, blindfolded Billy sitting in the middle, and the Dame with the cardboard plate the other side, she standing a bit upstage of Billy

(*To Billy*) Right, once again I'll ask you. What has that lady over there just picked up?
Billy (*still seated*) Er—er. . . .
Dame (*with the cardboard plate at the ready*) Well . . .?
Billy (*suddenly standing up, inspired*) I know! It's suddenly hit me!
Dame (*grimly*) It certainly will hit you—any moment now!

The Dame laughs, and Clarence laughs even more. The Dame moves back her arm ready to swing the slosh at Billy. As she moves the slosh forwards again, Billy suddenly sits down and the Dame puts the plate of slosh on to the laughing Clarence's face instead. Loud vaudeville music

Clarence (*shouting*) Hey! What d'you think you're doing! This is outrageous! I'm covered in custard!

Clarence chases the Dame off and Billy exits with the stool, laughing at them both. From the other side, the Princess enters

Princess (*to the audience*) Was that Silly Billy over there?
Audience Yes!
Princess Oh good. I want to ask him where Jack is. (*She crosses the stage calling*) Billy! Is that you Billy?

There is a dramatic music chord

Fleshcreep enters and bars her way

Fleshcreep Not so fast, my pretty Princess! You want to talk to Jack?
Princess Yes!
Fleshcreep I'm afraid that won't be possible, my dear.
Princess Why won't it be possible?
Fleshcreep My Master, the Giant . . .
Princess You and the Giant! What do you want *this* time?
Fleshcreep *You*, my dear.
Princess Get out of my sight you loathsome creature!
Fleshcreep You look very attractive when you're angry.
Princess That's no compliment coming from you!
Fleshcreep Pretty as a picture
Sweet as gooseberry pie
Just right for Giant Blunderbore
Way up in the sky!
Princess (*gasping*) What d'you mean? Oh please don't take me to the Giant, *please!*

Sinister music, as Fleshcreep puts out both his hands towards her, hypnotizing her

Fleshcreep Don't struggle 'cos my magic
Has got you in its sway
The Giant wants to meet you—
And he shall this very day!
Princess (*half asleep*) Don't take me to the Giant's Castle! Don't take me to Cloudland. Don't take me to the Giant . . .
Fleshcreep Let lightning flash
Let thunder roar
AWAY—TO GIANT BLUNDERBORE!

Walking backwards, Fleshcreep hypnotizes the Princess so that she has to follow right across the stage with the thunder and lightning effects. They exit. From the other side, the King runs in and daylight lighting returns

King (*to the audience*) What happened then? Was that my daughter?
Audience YES!
King With the Giant's Henchman?
Audience YES!
King Help! (*He calls out*) Town Crier! Town Crier!

Clarence, now without the tray, enters with his bell

Clarence Clarence Clanger here! What do you want me to do?
King Clang!
Clarence Right! (*He rings his bell*)

The Dame, Billy, Spick and Span—who salute—and the Townsfolk enter urgently

Billy Hullo, kids!

Audience Hullo, Billy!
King (*to everyone as they enter—in a great panic*) My daughter has been kidnapped by Fleshcreep!
All (*horrified*) Kidnapped?
King What are we going to do?
Dame (*dramatically pointing to it*) Look! The sword has been pulled out of the stone!

All react with amazement and pleasure

But who did it?

The Dame turns to the Townsfolk and others, but all shake their head, so she addresses the audience

Any of you see who pulled the magic sword out?
Audience Jack! It was Jack!
Dame (*thrilled*) *My* Jack?
Audience Yes!
Dame My Jack did it! (*In tears of emotion she calls out loudly and dramatically*) THIS MEANS MY JACK WILL BE JACK THE GIANT KILLER!!

All cheer. Black-out

If desired, a reprise of eight bars of an earlier up-tempo production number can be inserted between the cheer and the Black-out

Scene 4

On the Way Back to the Village

Tabs or a front-cloth of countryside and the path, or perhaps tabs which soon open to reveal a flat with a signpost on it. The one sign points one way and says "TO THE TOWN" and the other sign points the other way and says "TO THE VILLAGE"—or "TO THERE" and "AND BACK"
The trunk of a tree is put on stage during the Black-out

Flash! The Fairy enters R *and slowly crosses the stage as she tells of her problems*

Fairy My dears, Jack couldn't sell Daisy the Cow
So what does a fairy like me do now?
If *only* Jack was involved with flowers
Or vegetables or plants, my powers
Would then be strong, the boy I could nurture
But I'm only connected with horticulture!

She is much distressed and shakes her head

Magic powers! I haven't got any!
'Cos I'm only connected with Botany!

Oh, that Henchman is bad, with a cruel streak
To get through his defences I must find a leak!

She produces the large leek from behind her back

Oh! That's dandy and handy!
But if anything happens to do with a garden
Such as beans, or cucumber—*hic*—beg your pardon
I will repeat that: beans or cucumber,
Why then I attack, and I win, by thunder!

She waves her leek as a wand at this, but as nothing has happened, she looks round embarrassed

I'll say that again.
Why then I attack and I win, *by thunder!*

Tremendous loud thunder clap and noise from the percussion

That's the loudest noise I've heard in years!
Sounded like—(politician's name)—didn't it, my dears?

The Fairy exits. From other side, Fleshcreep enters to a dramatic chord

Fleshcreep For a nice country boy
The outlook is black
'Cos I'm going to destroy
Your young hero Jack!
Yes soon before your very eyes
I shall return—in a cunning disguise!
Ha ha ha ha ha ha!

Fleshcreep exits. From the other side, Jack enters with Daisy the Cow. The Cow moves to the tree trunk

Jack Hey-ho, Daisy, not much farther to go before we get home! After all this walking my feet are aching. It's time to sit down.

The Cow's hind part sits on the tree trunk, the fore part sits on the hind part and crosses its front legs

(*Laughing*) Hey! I mean it's time for *me* to sit down! Oh well, take the weight off your feet—I mean hooves.

The Cow makes herself comfortable by crossing her legs the other way, and nods her head with reactions to the following

I can't wait to see Mum's face when we get back. She'll be furious with me! But you know, Daisy, I never *really* wanted to sell you, so now we'll all be together again! You and me and Mum and Billy! *United* we stand, divided we fall!

Daisy moos

No, not United Dairies, silly!

There are sudden flashes of lightning, the stage darkens, mysterious music plays. Jack looks round anxiously. The Cow stands up from the log and moos

(*Looking round*) That's strange. The sun was shining when we left the Cattle Market and now there's thunder and it's gone dark! (*He shrugs*) Must be a summer storm.

Fleshcreep enters with a hooded cowl and voluminous cloak, or whatever seems right to disguise him as an old country woman. He bends double and shuffles and speaks with an old country woman's rustic accent

Fleshcreep Hullo, my dear, what a very fine cow!
Jack I'm taking her home, I must leave you now.
Fleshcreep One minute, dearie, I'm old and I'm grey
So let me have my final say.

The Cow reacts, jumping up and down, stamping feet and mooing

Jack Well we want to get home. We mustn't be rude,
But Daisy's already late for her food.
Fleshcreep She's a very fine cow, even though she's old.
So I'd like to buy her—
Jack Never!
Fleshcreep FOR A BAG OF GOLD!

Jack reacts, turns to the audience

Jack Did you hear that? A bag of gold! Oh she's a dear old country-woman but she's gone a bit soft in the head.
Fleshcreep (*holding up a bag*) Soft in the head dearie?
Jack (*taking the bag*) GOLD! (*He opens the bag wide so all the audience can see the gold, and drops the gold pieces back*)
Fleshcreep Yes, dearie, and what an incredible bargain! A cow in exchange for a bag of gold!
Jack It is an incredible bargain! (*To the audience*) Shall I sell Daisy?
Audience NO!
Jack Are you sure?
Audience NO!

The Cow shakes her head sadly

Jack (*overcome*) Oh Daisy . . . (*To the audience*) But what can I do? It's—gold! GOLD! (*To Fleshcreep*) I'll sell her.
Fleshcreep That's it, dearie, I knew you would. I've given you the gold, now give me the cow.

Jack hands over the rope

That's it, dearie. (*Sweetly*) Come on, Daisy, come to Granny.
Jack It's all right Daisy, she'll give you good food and a good time!
Fleshcreep (*eagerly*) I'll give her a good time all right! (*He pulls the Cow cruelly. At the exit*) That young man's not watching me now, so *take that!*

Fleshcreep hits the Cow hard with the rope's end and exits, dragging off the protesting Daisy while the audience boos him

Jack is so excited as he studies the gold that he does not see this cruelty

Up-tempo music starts

Jack (*to the audience*) Just think, this gold will buy us everything we ever wanted—a home for me and Mum and roller skates for Billy! And now I can marry my Princess! Oh, I'm so happy! I'm the happiest and richest man in the whole world!

Billy enters

Billy Hullo, kids!
Audience Hullo, Billy!
Billy (*to Jack*) I heard what you just said. So you've sold Daisy?
Jack (*showing him the gold*) Yes, for a fabulous bag of gold! Oh Billy, we're going to be rich! (*He sings*)

SONG 6

Either one song about money and becoming rich or a group of such songs. You may like Billy and Jack to do a vaudeville style song and dance here to end the scene with a vaudeville exit

At the end of the song there is a Black-out

Scene 5

INSIDE DAME TROT'S COTTAGE

See Scenery Notes. This scene "transforms" later

It is evening, dim lighting

The Dame is in a dressing-gown and frilly nightcap or a wig with curlers

Dame (*with comedy pacing to and fro*) Where is Jack? Why is he so late? I wonder if he's sold Daisy? I wonder how much he's got for her? Oh, I shall go mad, waiting like this!

The King enters

King Dame Trot! (*As she does not hear*) Trotty!
Dame Kingy! Hullo!
King (*with a big roguish smile*) Hullo!
Dame (*to the audience*) When he smiles like that he wants something—and I'll tell you this, he's not going to get it.
King Yes I *do* want something.
Dame (*flinging her arms back and sticking out her chest*) Take me—(*some romantic film name*)—I'm yours!
King I want the rent.
Dame (*coming down to earth*) What?

King I'm sorry, Mrs Trot, but I've got to have the rent because I've got to pay the Giant Tax. I'm very sorry. (*Calling off*) Sergeant Spick and Corporal Span, quick march!

Spick and Span march in, turn to the front and salute together—Spick salutes with his right hand correctly, but Span salutes with his left

Dame It's no use bringing in the Royal Guardsmen. I can't pay the rent. I've no money and I've nothing out in the farmyard.

King
Spick
Span } Nothing? { (*Speaking together*)

Dame Nothing.
King But where's the hen?
Dame Gone.
Spick And where's the bull?
Dame Gone.
Span And where's the duck?
Dame Gone.
King But this used to be a beautiful farm with lots of animals!
Dame That's when Old Macdonald had it. Shall I tell you about it?

King
Spick
Span } (*groaning*) NO. { (*Speaking together*)

Dame All right, then I will. (*She sings at a brisk tempo*)

SONG 7 OLD MACDONALD HAD A FARM

Old Macdonald had a farm
Eeee aye eee aye oh.
And on that farm he had a bull
Eeee aye eee aye oh.
With a mooo-mooo here
A mooo-mooo there
Here a mooo, there a mooo,
Everywhere a mooo-mooo
Old Macdonald had a farm
Eeee aye eee aye oh!

She sings it fast, in fact the accompaniment can be "cha cha" tempo or even "rock" and the audience is persuaded to clap. As each person does his or her solo the others do a square dance with emphatic music tempo. The King sings equally fast because this song is fun but it must not drag. He mentions that Macdonald had a Duck, with a quack quack here and a quack there, etc. and the Dame joins him in the roundelay

Not only should the song be sung fast, but some comedy choreography is needed so that those who are not singing are not standing doing nothing. They can bend their knees in time, or do the rock 'n' roll hand movements with clenched fists or—as mentioned—a square dance. If desired, Silly Billy and Clarence Clanger can enter and join in and the lyric is extended for them

King With a quack here,
A quack quack there,
Here a quack, there a quack,
Everywhere a quack quack—
Dame With a moo moo here
A moo moo there
Here a moo, there a moo
Everywhere a mooo-mooo
Both Old Macdonald had a farm
Eeee aye eee aye oh!

Sergeant Spick sings, fast, that Old Macdonald had a dog, with a woof woof here, etc. and is then joined by the King, then the Dame and then all sing the last two lines

Corporal Span sings, fast, that Old Macdonald had a sow and they end the song as fast as possible, it does not matter that it is a jumble and they get in a muddle. Nor does it matter if the audience joins or claps—in fact, the more they do the better. Each chorus is taken up a key. The final chorus is as follows

King With a quack quack here
A quack quack there
Here a quack, there a quack
Everywhere a quack quack—
Dame With a moo moo here
A moo moo there
Here a moo, there a mooo
Everywhere a mooo-moooo—
Spick With a woof woof here
A woof woof there
Here a woof, there a woof
Everywhere a woof woof—
Span With an oik oik here
An oik oik there
Here an oik, there an oik,
Everywhere an oik oik—

They all four sing a grand finale ending

All Old Macdonald had a farm
Eeee—aye
Eeee—aye
Oh!

After the comedy song all exit in big vaudeville style, waving their arms. From the other side, Jack enters with the bag of gold. He moves downstage

Jack (*calling excitedly*) Mum! Where is she . . . Mum! Fabulous news, Mum! *Mum!*

The Dame enters

Dame (*excitedly and eagerly*) Hullo, dear!
Jack (*remaining downstage*) Hullo, Mum!
Dame (*impatiently*) Well, tell me what happened! (*She puts out her hands, twitching with anticipation*)
Jack How are you?
Dame What do you mean, how are you? Have you sold the cow?
Jack (*very pleased with himself*) Yes I've sold the cow.
Dame *Well?*
Jack What do you mean, well?
Dame I'm going mad. *What did you get for the cow?*
Jack Guess. Was it five pounds? No. Was it three pounds? No. Then what was it we ask ourselves.
Dame My nerves won't stand much more of this. WHAT DID YOU GET FOR THE COW?
Jack A bag of gold.
Dame Ah good . . . (*A huge reaction*) A bag of gold?

Jack scoops coins out of the bag, drops a gold coin as he says each word of the following clearly showing the audience the gold. The Dame does not see this however

Jack A—bag—of—GOLD!
Dame Gold! Oh my boy, that's wonderful. Show me!

She moves to him so that they are both C. *Jack holds out the open bag for the Dame to see—but they both freeze as statues. Mysterious music*

Fleshcreep enters L *and addresses the audience*

Fleshcreep Gold? Huh! She'll wonder what Jack means.
For watch—I'll turn the gold into *beans*!

(*He waves his hand towards the bag*)

Chord of mysterious music

The Fairy enters R, *pleased at the cue of the word "beans"*

Fairy BEANS! I'm the Fairy of Vegetables and Flowers
So at last I *can* use my magic powers!
To help you Jack, that was my pledge
And now I *can* help—for beans are veg!

But Fleshcreep is withering

Fleshcreep Beans—Jack is *ruined*. Oh aren't I clever!

Fleshcreep exits triumphantly L

Fairy BEANS! THEY SHALL MAKE JACK FAMOUS FOR EVER!

The Fairy exits triumphantly R

The Dame and Jack come to life again

Dame (*putting her hand into the bag*) Gold! Oh Nicholas Parsons, it's the Sale of the Century! Oh we'll be rich and . . . (*After a horrified pause*) Just a minute. This isn't gold, it's *beans!*

Jack What? What are you talking about, Mother?
Dame They're beans! Look! Oh Jack, what have you done? A bag of beans in exchange for Daisy! We're ruined! We'll be the laughing stock of the neighbourhood!
Jack But Mum, it was gold when I got it!
Dame Gold? What are you talking about you foolish boy!
Jack But it *was* gold—it was!
Dame (*furiously*) Now you've really spilt the beans.
Jack But . . .
Dame (*shouts*) Silence! Out of the window they go, out into the vegetable patch where they belong!

In her fury, the Dame throws the beans out of the window. There is a flash outside the window area

(*Pathetically, no comedy*) Oh Jack we're finished—finished! We've lost Daisy so we've lost everything! You naughty boy, get to bed! (*She cries, with convulsive sobs*) Oh—oh—oh.
Jack Mum, I'm sorry. I'm truly sorry. If I can explain . . .
Dame (*shouts*) BED!
Jack (*defeated—it is a tragedy*) Yes, Mum . . .

To a few bars of sad music the Dame and Jack exit on opposite sides, in the the deepest despair. The Fairy enters downstage, as optimistic as ever

Fairy It's night and now they've gone to bed
But when the sun shines overhead
When we see tomorrow's morning
What a day for Jack is dawning!

She waves her wand over the scene, there is mysterious fairy music

TRANSFORMATION SCENE

See the scenery notes for the Beanstalk growing

As the Cottage is removed and the Beanstalk grows the Fairy speaks

The beans the Dame threw from her hand
Possess the power that I command!
Here from this spot a magic plant shall rise
Whose boughs shall form a ladder to the skies!

The Magic People dressed as beans or insects or fairies or butterflies, etc., enter after the Beanstalk Growing Effect, as SCENE 6 *opens*

SCENE 6

BEANSTALKLAND UP IN THE CLOUDS

The Cottage has been removed, the Beanstalk has been seen to grow, and a backcloth of entwined beanstalk is now in place, with Beanstalk wings

SONG 8

SHORT DANCE ROUTINE/BALLET

During this routine, Fleshcreep enters and drags the fiercely struggling Princess across the stage and exits with her

If the two who are in the cow costume are not needed in the Transformation, then for story reasons it is nice if Fleshcreep drags the Princess with one hand and holds the rope with the Cow with the other and drags them both across the stage

After the routine there is a fanfare

The Fairy enters triumphantly, holding a sword, and she ushers in Jack—who now wears Transformation Scene armour, or a splendid hat and cloak over his former costume

Fairy Now, Jack you are my champion
And with your magic sword
You'll fight the wicked Giant
And gain Love's sweet reward!

She hands Jack the sword, which he dramatically points upwards to the sky

Jack This is where my adventures begin
I'm going to fight the Giant—*AND WIN!*

All dramatically sing eight bars of some reprise from Act One
Finally, all group on either side of Jack, who takes up a dramatic pose for the—

GRAND TABLEAU

On the last note of the routine—

the CURTAIN *falls*

ACT II

Scene 1

THE DRAGON'S CAVE OUTSIDE THE GIANT'S CASTLE

There are rocks and stones on a big scale and we can see the top of the Beanstalk sticking up from behind an upstage ground row of rocks. Perhaps we can see clouds and the Giant's Castle in the distance. In the taller rocks at the side, there is a fairly big jagged opening to a cave which leads off

SONG 9 (*see Musical Numbers at beginning of script*)

During the routine, Fleshcreep drags across the fiercely struggling Princess—and maybe Daisy the Cow also

After the Dance Routine or Production Number, the spooky animals or Villager/prisoners exit

Comedy sinister music is heard, and a strange old hag—a French Revolution Tricoteuse with blacked out teeth and rags—hobbles in, cackling and muttering loudly

Mrs Blunderbore (*looking round quirkily and cackling, then addressing the audience*) Ha ha ha ha ha! I must introduce myself. I am the Giant's wife—yes, I'm Mrs Blodwyn Blunderbore! I've had a terrible time since I married the Giant. To look at me you'd never know I was only twenty-one, now would you? I used to be such a pretty gel before the Giant married me. Yes, I was known as the Mary Poppins of—(*local joke place*). But *now*, I'm cunning and cruel and crafty. (*She venemously points to the top of the Beanstalk*) Curses! There's the magic Beanstalk—that means people are going to *climb* up that Beanstalk from the village down below! *I must watch out for them.* Then I shall GRAB them—(*she claws the air in a menacing way*)—and give them to the Giant and he will EAT them! (*She cackles*) Ha ha ha ha ha!

There is a loud dragon roar on the offstage microphone

(*Moving to the wings*) Ooooooh, that's the Giant's dreadful dragon, and he wants his elevenses! It's time for the Dragon's tea break! (*She collects a three-foot high cut-out of a petrol tin marked "PETROL"*) I'll give him some gunpowder soup and T.N.T. pudding—and instead of coffee he likes a couple of tins of petrol—well dragons need petrol, they need it for the *flames*, you see! (*She cackles*) Ha ha ha ha ha! Yes, he needs it for the flames that come out of his great big ghastly gaping mouth! (*She calls*) Coming, my pet! Coming, dearie! Ha ha ha ha ha!

Mrs Blunderbore hobbles off into the cave and exits, cackling like crazy

Comedy spooky music

The Dame, the King, Billy, Clarence the Town Crier, Sergeant Spick and Corporal Span—who salute as usual—all creep on in single file, looking round—terrified. If possible, they enter in the Beanstalk area as though they have just climbed up it

The Dame turns to the King with finger to her lips and she says a loud "Sssh!" The King does the same to Billy and then they "Sssh" all the way down the line. When this business reaches Span at the end of the line, he turns to say "Ssssh!" to someone, finds there's no-one there, so quickly runs round the back of the line and pops up by the Dame. He says "Sssh!" to her and she again says "Ssssh!" to the King, and the "Sssh" goes all the way down the line again, then Spick finds there's no one there so runs down the back of the line to Span and goes "Sssh". But when Span turns and goes "Sssh!" to the Dame she realizes what is happening

Dame (*hitting Span*) Stop it! (*Looking round*) So this is the Land of the Jolly Green Giant!
Mrs Blunderbore (*cackling on the offstage microphone*) Ha ha ha ha!

Everyone freezes with terror and gasps and looks round

Dame Wazzat?
Billy It's Dirty Gertie from Number Thirty!
King (*slowly and loudly*) Shush! Shush!
Dame (*reciting loudly*) Whisper who dares, Christopher Robin likes chocolate eclairs! (*She laughs hilariously*) Ha ha ha ha!
All QUIET.
Dame (*stops laughing*) Pardon.
Clarence (*to Billy*) Are you frightened?
Billy Frightened? I'm not frightened. I'm *terrified.*
King (*to the Dame*) But *you're* not scared are you?
Dame (*bravely, but in an odd position caused by terror*) *No!*
King Then why are you standing like that?
Dame I've got my knickers in a twist.

Percussion noises as the Dame does some contortions to straighten herself

That's better.

Percussion "blocks" are heard

Billy Listen! (*He and the King listen*) What's that nun-nun-nun knocking?
King (*shaking at the knees*) It's my nun-nun-nun-knees!

Span suddenly stands rigidly to attention and goggles his eyes

Spick What's the matter with you?
Span I'm scared stiff! (*He starts to keel over and wails*) Aaaaow!
Spick (*scratching his head*) Another fine mess you've got me into, Olly!
Dame I've just had a marvellous idea! We're all scared out of our minds so why don't we sing!

They all clear their throats and sing

SONG 10

As they sing, Mrs Blunderbore hobbles out of the cave, sees them and puts up her claw like hands in a menacing position and cackles

As they continue to sing the audience shouts out their warnings

Mrs Blunderbore soon scares off—in turn—Spick, Span, Clarence and then, from the other side of the line up, the King and the Dame

Mrs Blunderbore and Silly Billy are left together. They both sing away happily and the audience will be shouting advice. She does not look at Billy. He turns to her, then looks at the audience and realizes what he has seen, so he pulls a face of terror

Billy (*calling out over her singing*) What a horrible old hag! I must scare her away! (*An idea*) I know! (*He takes from his pocket a hideous Dracula-style mask made of rubber and holds it in front of his face and stares at her, letting out a hideous scream*)

Mrs Blunderbore (*romantically clutching her chest*) Oh! Roger Moore! Oh, Engelbert Humperdinck! Take me, I'm yours!

Billy (*shouting*) Help!

Mrs Blunderbore chases Billy off to vaudeville music, and both exit. Fairy music as the Fairy enters from the other side, ushering Jack in his Transformation Scene costume and carrying his sword

Jack Good Fairy, we've reached the Citadel!

Fairy (*to the audience*) And didn't he do well?

Jack gazes round

Jack So there is Castle Blunderbore. . . .

Fairy Yes, Jack—but hark, the dragon's roar!

During her last speech a loud roar is heard on the offstage microphone and it scares her greatly

Jack The dragon? That's put me in a spot.

Fairy In my euphoria I clean forgot
To tell you about the dragon's cave!
But you'll win through. You're strong and brave!

The thunderous dragon sounds on the offstage microphone are heard. Dramatic music. The Fairy reacts with terror

Ooooooo! How the mighty monster roared!
But remember, Jack, you've the magic sword!
Cut into the skin, all scaly and thick—
As for me—I'm going to exit—*quick!*

The Fairy exits

Loud dramatic music, thunder, lightning flashes, percussion noises, all very frightening. Jack is waiting tensed

All the dramatic effects of roars and very loud Wagnerian music and thunder and lightning suddenly stop as the attractive little Dragon enters. It waddles happily downstage as Jack addresses it

Jack (*greatly surprised*) Hey! You don't look scary to me! I was told you were fearful, frightful and awful. But you're cuddly, cheerful and chubby! I think you must be a magic dragon! (*To the audience*) There are such things you know. (*He clicks his fingers*) Wait a minute! I've just realized who you are! (*He sings*)

SONG 11

As Jack sings, the Dragon waddles about and waves its arms in time to the music, and Jack gets the audience to join each chorus
After the song the Lights Black-out

Scene 2

THE HENCHMAN'S EVIL GROTTO IN THE CASTLE

Tabs, or a front-cloth of a spooky and sinister room-cum-grotto. There are enormous Giant chains hanging down and huge spiked clubs and shields and rough furniture. Maybe a barred window; in fact, it is an eerie place painted to the huge Giant Blunderbore scale with plenty of cobwebs. To one side, unnoticed and out of the way, is a dark-coloured chest

Dramatic music, thunder and lightning as the Villagers enter cowering and crying out with a rope from one girl's wrist to the next man to the next girl and so on down the line as though a chain gang. Fleshcreep follows them on, lashing out with his whip at the stragglers

Villagers Don't hit us! We're the prisoners of the Giant! Take pity on us!

Fleshcreep (*whipping them*) Get on! I haven't got all day! Onwards to the dungeons!

First Villager (*turning round and daring to call out to Fleshcreep*) Stop this cruelty, you stupid great bully!

Fleshcreep *What* did you say?

First Villager I said . . .

Fleshcreep (*evilly*) I heard what you said. And for that you shall *all* suffer. When you get to the dungeons I'll play you the new Des O'Connor record—(*or a contemporary pop star*)

All (*crying out*) No—spare us! Not that, please not that!

Girl Villager Please! I appeal to you!

Fleshcreep You don't appeal to me one bit. You're just a puny peasant! (*Lashing out with the whip*) *Hah!*

Second Villager (*defiantly*) You can't do this to us! We'd rather starve to death!

Fleshcreep Good. Because I was going to give you all bread and water but instead I'll give you bread and *liquid paraffin!* Ha ha ha ha!

All Mercy! Have pity on us!

Third Villager (*bravely*) We're going to rebel! And *I'm* going to lead the rebellion!

Fleshcreep (*pointing his whip at this villager*) If you do I'll take you to the torture chamber and I'll tie you up to the Iron Lady!

Third Villager (*petrified*) No—not Margaret Thatcher!

Fleshcreep Silence fool! Onwards all of you, onwards!

He lashes out at them and they start to exit the other side

Villagers No! No!
Help us someone!
We're doomed! Doomed!
What a fate we have to suffer!
If only we could escape!
Show mercy, please show mercy!
Woe! Oh woe!

Fleshcreep (*pointing off*) There's the door to the dungeon—just there. In you go, you mouldy mortals! Into the dark and dismal dungeon! That's it! In you go! Ha ha ha ha!

Fleshcreep whips them and they exit. He is about to follow but the Fairy enters from the other side

Fairy (*calling cheekily*) Hey! Ugly!

Fleshcreep (*incredulously*) *Ugly?* (*He turns back and sees her*) Oh, it's you! (*He recites*)
Why are you here, you Fairy fey
It's my home, where I live, it's my grotto!

Fairy Well if you live here then all I can say
Is no wonder you're practicall\ blotto!

Fleshcreep Haven't you noticed my magical spells?

Fairy So far all I've noticed are horrible smells!
I've never met anyone so uncouth
This pace needs some Airwick, and that's the truth!

Fleshcreep Silence! For magic you need a room
That is cold and dark and full of gloom.
That's why my magic is so much stronger.

Fairy I'm not listening to you any longer

Fleshcreep My magic's *superb!* It's *powerful!* It's *strong!*

Fairy *No!* Listen to me while I tell you *in song!*

She sings

SONG 12

This duet is a challenge and each sings a short chorus. The Fairy, R, *starts and during it she waves her wand and from the wings at her side a big bright coloured cut-out of a daisy-style flower is stuck out from the wings. When Fleshcreep,* L, *sings his short chorus he makes magic passes at his side wings and out shoots a cut-out hammer instead of a flower. It comes down on his head and hits him—percussion effect. On his last note, he seems to be winning this "song competition" but a very large three-foot carrot either falls from above or is thrown from the wings at him and the Fairy takes over the last notes as she is "the winner"*

On the last notes, the Fairy exits R, *triumphantly waving her wand and Fleshcreep staggers off* L, *groaning and holding his head. Comedy spooky music is heard, as the Dame and the King creep in* R

Dame (*looking round*) Isn't it dark? Have you got ten p for the meter?
King (*also looking round*) It *is* dark. (*Comically lecherous*) I've wanted to get you into a dark room for a long time and this *is* a dark room.
Dame Then what are you waiting for?
King To see if anything develops.
Dame (*enjoying herself, coyly*) Oh Mr King, I bet you say that to all the girls.
King Only to you, because you're a poppet. (*He kneels down on both knees*) My poppet! My poppet! My poppet!
Dame Poppet? (*She pushes him away*) Stop it or you'll cop it!

She moves away several paces. He follows her across the stage, still on his knees

King Kiss me.
Dame But I've never kissed a man before!
King Neither have I, so don't let that stop you. (*He stands up and embraces her*)
Dame (*struggling*) No! Desist!
King Desist?
Dame Desist—I insist—I don't want to be kissed—(*snatching away her hand*)—and let go of my wrist!
King (*formally*) Mrs Trot, may I kiss your hand?
Dame Why, is my face dirty? (*To the audience*) The man's drunk. (*To the King*) What's the matter with you?
King Dear lady, in your hands I'm a hot-water tap.
Dame (*much surprised*) A hot-water tap?
King You turn me on.
Dame (*pleased*) Silly boy.
King You little raver. (*Passionately*) I go for you! I go for you!
Dame Why can't you go for yourself?
King Mrs Trot, you must be more romantic than this. Don't you realize, I'm King Satupon and I love you!
Dame (*to the audience, thrilled*) Oh! Oh me jam tart! It's the King and I!

They sing and dance

SONG 13

As they dance they suddenly stop

OW! You hit my hand!
King (*with a little head bow*) I'll kiss it better.

He kisses her hand, they continue to dance, then stop again

Dame Ow! You hit my foot!
King (*with a little bow*) I'll kiss it better.

He kneels down, kisses her toe, then they continue to dance, and turn back to back

(*Romantically*) I love dancing cheek to cheek.
Dame Ow! You hit my bottom!
King (*with a little bow*) I'll kiss it bet . . . (*He realizes*) I think I'll let that get better on its own!

This is almost at the end of the duet, and on the last note of the song. The Dame and the King exit. Spooky music, as the Fairy enters with Jack, who holds the sword

Jack The Giant and his Henchman are unaware
We've reached their castle in the air!
The Giant my plans shall not forestall!

The Fairy listens to her hero, nodding enthusiastically. Now she gets over-enthusiastic and waves her wand

Fairy Oh Cinderella, you SHALL go to the ball!
What am I saying? Wrong pantomime!
(*Concerned*) Are you tired after the beanstalk climb?
Jack When I need my Princess? Good heavens no!
This is adventure! I'm all set to go!
You and I will be in danger
But danger is to me no stranger!
Fairy Oh you'll be all right, you're proud and haughty
But what about me—I'm over forty!

Jack does dramatic actions with his sword and paces about

Jack I'll chop the Giant's head off quick as a trice!
But first, I expect you've got some advice?
Fairy Yes, I *have*, actually . . .
I know to get at the Giant you're itchin'
But first, let me show you the Giant's kitchen.

They huddle together while she points off and speaks with emphasis

Now he sleeps after dinner and that is when
You must grab the magic hen
That lays the golden egg—

Jack is enthusiastic, starts to move on, sword at the ready, but the Fairy holds him back

Jack Yes!
Fairy *No*. For stay.
Just as you are creeping away
His singing harp will scream and shout

Then he'll awake, and you'll get such a clout! (*She waves her wand*)
His cudgel is covered with spikes and nails
And you know what a clout with *that* entails!

Jack You mean blood all over me I shall get!

Fairy And the National Health's not been invented yet!

Jack Oh thank you Fairy, I'm sure I'll win through.

Fairy Watch out for that cudgel whatever you do.

Jack Goodness and honesty I will defend!

Fairy Well said, my boy. (*Proud of him, to the audience*)
Oh he'll win through in the end!
When the Giant waves his cudgel and you have to duck
Well—I wish you the best of British luck!

The Fairy, ever optimistic exits

Jack So I go down the passage and find the door
That leads to the horrible Blunderbore
I'll then kill the Giant and with that success
I'll finally rescue my own dear Princess!

On the heroically spoken last line, Jack waves his sword and exits. From the other side, Fleshcreep drags the Princess on

Fleshcreep I've got some news for you—the Giant *likes* you. He thinks you're a choice morsel. He thinks you're a dish—and the dish will be Princess Pie!

Princess One day you'll pay for this. You're Count Dracula and Frankenstein rolled into one!

Fleshcreep Flattery will get you nowhere. Mind you, I like women to have spirit.

Princess Well I like a man to have a bath. You haven't had a bath in years, you loathsome lout!

Fleshcreep I like the way you said that. I'll come to a little arrangement with you—I'll keep you away from the Giant and keep you *for myself*.

The Giant roars on the offstage microphone and startles Fleshcreep

Giant (*off*) Fee Fi Fo Fum
I smell the blood of an Englishman
Be he alive or be he dead
I'll grind his bones to make my bread.

Over the voice of the Giant, Fleshcreep speaks

Fleshcreep (*scared*) I must go and tell my master I've brought you to the castle! You stay here, or straightaway you'll be put into a pie—and eaten! Ha ha ha! (*He calls*) Coming master!

Fleshcreep exits

Princess Thank goodness the Giant's Henchman has left me alone! At least I'm free to wander about this horrible place—and I'm free to think about Jack . . . (*She sees the chest at the side of the stage, sits on it and sings*)

SONG 14

(*After the song*) It's a curious old chest. I wonder what's inside it? (*She stands up and examines it*) What's this? On the lid it says "The Golden Sticks—do not touch". (*To the audience*) Shall I open the box?

Audience Yes!

Princess I wonder what's in it? (*She takes out three gold bits of wood and is puzzled*) Three gold sticks! They're like a jig-saw puzzle!

Giant (*off*, *roaring*) Fee fi fo fum!

Princess (*scared*) The Giant! That means the Henchman will soon be back! But these sticks—I'm sure they're somehow connected with my fate in this horrible castle. I must hide them!

Giant (*off*) Ho ho ho! I smell the blood of an English girl!

Princess (*looking round desperately*) But there's nowhere to hide them! Unless—will *you* look after them for me? (*She moves to the stage steps and appeals to the audience*)

Audience Yes!

Princess (*looking back at the stage*) No-one's coming! So here—you take one! (*She runs down fast into the stalls and hands out the three gold sticks, thanking the children*)

Giant (*off*) Fee fi fo fum!

Princess (*to the audience*, *terrified*) I must get back! You *will* guard them for me, won't you?

Audience (*particularly the three children*) Yes!

The Princess scrambles quickly back on to the stage

As she is doing so, Fleshcreep enters

Fleshcreep What were you doing down there?

Princess Nothing! (*To the audience*) I wasn't doing anything, was I?

Audience No!

Fleshcreep All right, then. I thought for a moment you were. Here, what's this? (*He sees the open box*) Have you opened the box?

Princess Box, what box?

Fleshcreep runs to her and grabs her arm. She struggles

Fleshcreep Don't you play the innocent with me! You little vixen, you've stolen the golden sticks!

Princess Sticks! What sticks? What are you talking about?

Fleshcreen (*scared*) If the Giant finds the magic sticks are missing, he'll grind *my* bones to make his bread! I'm frightened—really frightened! (*To the audience*) I appeal to you my friends! If I don't find the magic sticks the Giant will punish me and you wouldn't like that would you?

Audience Yes!

Fleshcreep You insolent dogs! Where are the sticks?

Princess (*aside to the audience*) Don't tell him, please don't tell him!

Giant (*off*) Fleshcreep! Come here, Fleshcreep! Ho ho ho!

Fleshcreep (*terrified*) The Giant! We must go! (*He pushes the Princess into the wings*)

The Princess exits

(*To the audience*) One more time—have you got the golden sticks. You've been helping the Princess, haven't you?

Audience NO!

Fleshcreep Very well. Here is my curse! I'm going to bite the heads off all your Cindy dolls! I'm going to smash your Video Games—and why not? The Giant has smashed mine! (*He calls*) Coming, oh Master! *Coming, J.R.—(or whoever is a topical villain)*

Fleshcreep exits, to dramatic chords

The Lights immediately come up to full, as the tabs open or the front-cloth is flown

Scene 3

THE GIANT'S KITCHEN

The scenery is to the big scale of the Giant, so is the furniture such as the Giant's chair and table, each about six foot high, which are up C. *The front of the Giant's table is mainly solid and on this solid boarding is a big heraldic shield that has three practical clips on it. It is pivoted on to the boarding so that it can revolve about ninety degrees. At one wing there is a great big seven-foot-high pepper pot marked "PEPPER", and at the other wing there is a great big hot-water bottle. This need not be practical. It can be painted on at the inside edge of the wing where all the audience can see it. Painted on the two wings and the backcloth are kitchen utensils such as a huge sweeping-brush, with handle leaning against the wall, huge onions on a string, huge cheese, open box of matches, a huge bottle of washing-up liquid, a kettle, frying-pan, a saucepan—none of these things need be practical but the audience will enjoy their big scale*

Mrs Blunderbore is waving a huge fork about four-foot high, and urging in the Villagers, prodding them with the fork

Mrs Blunderbore (*over the introduction music*) Come on you stupid earthlings! Hurry up, you horrible humans! Get the Giant's food ready or I'll take you back to the dungeons. Food! Food! (*She cackles*) Ha ha ha!

The Villagers, in chefs' hats and aprons bring into the kitchen huge plates of prop meat and fruit, a massive bottle marked "H.P. Sauce", cutlery and an enormous chain of sausages (these can all be cut-outs). Mrs Blunderbore stands at the side calling out instructions

Put that down there—take that to the pantry—shove that in the fridge —put that on the shelf, etc.

The audience likes it if she is made the central person of this Production Number (if she is a singer) and she of course remains in character as she sings and parades about like a "Broadway Musical Comedy Star gone a bit wrong". Or she conducts the song with the huge fork as she stands at the side of the stage and watches the Routine

SONG 15

After the song and dance, all exit, including Mrs Blunderbore

Comedy spooky music

The Dame, the King and Billy enter, creeping in

At once they hear the very loud thud—thud—thud of footsteps coming nearer

Billy (*shaking*) It's the Giant!
Dame (*shaking*) Or Fleshcreep!
Billy It's getting nearer!
Dame And nearer!
Billy / **Dame** Help! (*Cowering down together*) (*Speaking together*)

The King enters carrying a baby doll that has a frilly baby cap and a nappy that can easily be taken off the doll all in one piece and then later put on it again

King Oh there you are! Look what I've found in the Giant's pantry—this lovely baby!
Dame / **Billy** Aaaaaah . . . (*Speaking together*)
King The Giant was going to eat it—I just rescued it in time! You can look after it while I go and try to find my dear daughter.
Billy Look after it? I know nothing about babies!
King No, but Dame Trot does. She looked after you when you were a baby.
Dame Yes I did. But that was thirty-nine years ago.
Billy Twenty-nine, please!
King Oh don't be silly, Mrs Trot. Of course you can remember how to look after a baby.
Dame I tell you I can't, I *can't*.
King You don't have to know anything. All you need to do is bath it, feed it—and above all *keep it warm.*
Billy (*vaguely*) Keep it warm?
King Oh yes, that's very important. (*Emphatically*) You must keep it warm because that makes it grow.

The King hands the baby doll to Billy who awkwardly takes it

The King exits

Dame / **Billy**
You must keep it warm because that makes it grow.
You must keep it warm because that makes it grow.
You must keep it warm because . . . (*Speaking together*)

On the offstage microphone, there are earsplittingly loud comedy crying noises which continue

Baby AAAAAAAH!
Billy (*dithering and calling out over the baby's crying*) What'll I do with it?
Dame (*calling out also*) Don't ask me!
Billy But how can I stop it crying?
Dame Bung it up!
Billy (*disgusted*) Bung it up?
Dame You know—what you call it—what d'you call that thing you put in its mouth?
Billy A lollipop?
Dame No, er . . .
Billy Bubblegum?
Dame No, er . . .
Billy Gobstopper?
Dame No, no, er—er . . . (*To the audience*) Honestly, I can't remember a thing about bringing up babies, isn't it awful!
Billy (*taking a big dummy from where it is tucked into its nappy*) Dummy!
Dame Don't you call me a dummy. Me, your mother, who's worked her fingers to the bone for you morning noon and . . .
Billy (*holding it up*) Dummy!
Dame Oh.

Billy, with a big gesture, makes out he is putting the dummy in the baby's mouth, and instantly the baby crying noises stop with a gulp on the offstage microphone

Then I think I used to sing to it.
Billy *Sing* to it? With your voice?
Dame Yes. A lullaby.
Billy (*handing the baby doll to the Dame*) Oh Gawd! All right.

The Dame holds the Baby and sings as she rocks it in her arms

Dame Sweetest little fellow
Everybody knows
Don't know what to call him . . .

She pulls a face, realizing that The Worst has happened and sings the last line in an embarrassed way

But I'll have to change his clothes.
Billy I think the little thing should have a bath.
Dame (*unhappily*) Well *I'm* having a bath, believe me!

Billy reaches under the Giant's table and brings out a baby's bath and jug in it and pulls it downstage

Billy (*pointing to the bath*) It's dry.
Dame (*looking at the baby*) It's *dry?* You must be joking!
Billy I'll pour some water in.

Billy "pours water" from the empty jug and we hear some water-pouring effect on the offstage microphone or from the percussion. The Dame pulls the nappy from off the doll, puts the doll in the bath and the nappy on the floor

Dame (*to the baby*) Who's a lovely little boy!
Billy It's a girl.
Dame I told you my memory was going.
Billy (*waving his fingers at the baby doll that is now in the bath*) Coochie coo!
Dame Now, I remember the water's got to be lukewarm.
Billy Well, that lukes warm.

More loud baby crying noises on the offstage microphone

Dame (*to the baby*) All right, dear! She doesn't like the water.

Billy takes the baby out of the bath again

Billy And babies need *iron*, don't they?

Billy holds the baby while the Dame takes a big iron from the bath and starts to "iron" the baby's back and bottom

And I expect it wants its bottle.
Dame Oh yes!

She collects a big gin bottle marked "GIN" from the bath, puts it to the baby doll's mouth and we hear glug-glug-glug drinking noises at the offstage microphone

Now pat it for me. Go on, wind it!

Billy pats the doll's back and we hear a loud hiccup/burp on the offstage microphone

(*Reacting*) Manners!
Billy And now we've got to keep the baby *warm.*
Dame Otherwise it won't grow. I'll tidy up.

Billy holds out the baby and she puts the nappy on the baby again. Then she starts to put the various props back into the bath, not looking at Billy during this

Billy Oh, I've been left holding the baby. And we've got to keep the baby *warm* . . . (*To the audience*) What's warm in a horrible place like this?
Audience Hot-water bottle!
Billy What? Hot-water bottle? Where? (*Following their shouts*) Oh yes! The Giant's hot-water bottle! (*He pats the bottle painted on the scenery*) Oh and it's nice and warm—thanks! I'll put the baby by the hot-water bottle!

He puts the baby doll down behind the huge hot-water bottle, so that it is now out of sight behind the scenery wing

Dame (*with head turned away as she hands the bath off*) You keeping it warm?
Billy Oh yes!
Dame (*still not looking*) That's right then, dear . . .

The King enters

King I can't find my daughter anywhere. Well! I see you managed all right!

Dame
Billy } Oh yes! { (*Speaking together*)

King Did you bath the baby?

Dame
Billy } Oh yes! { (*Speaking together*)

King Did you feed it?

Dame
Billy } Oh yes! { (*Speaking together*)

King Did you keep it warm?

Billy Oh yes, we kept it warm!

King That's good! Did you put it to bed?

Dame No, I don't think so.

King Then what *did* you do with it?

Billy I put it by the hot-water bottle

King (*surprised*) By the hot-water bottle?

Dame
Billy } You must keep it warm because that makes it grow! { (*Speaking together*)

There is a crash from percussion

One of the male Singers jumps on stage from behind the hot-water bottle area wearing just a big baby's frilly bonnet and a big sort of nappy made of towels, and perhaps waving a big rattle

Baby (*with arms outstretched*) Mammy!

The Baby chases the Dame, Billy and the King off to loud vaudeville music, and all four exit. Jack enters from the other side to mysterious music

Jack (*in a half-whisper*) So this is the Giant's Kitchen, but where is the Giant? *And where's my Princess?* I've got to find her! The good fairy says she's in *here*, not in the dungeon. But where? (*Moving round the room*) There's the Giant's chair and his table, *but where's the Princess?* (*As he searches he looks off*) Oh, there's Billy. (*He calls*) Hey!

Billy enters

Billy You're safe! But what's the matter?

Jack I'm looking for the Princess! The Fairy told me she'd be here in the Giant's Kitchen but she's not!

Billy Well we can always have a search.

They both look round, and Billy points to the shield on the front of the Giant's table

Oh look—a dartboard!

Jack That's not a dartboard you chump, it's a shield! (*Curiously*) And it's got three clips on it! I wonder what they're for?

Billy It's like a jig-saw puzzle.

Jack (*to the audience*) Anyone see any bits of wood or three sticks? You have?
Audience YES!
Billy You mean, you're looking after them?
Audience Yes!

Billy and Jack go down into the audience and collect the gold sticks chatting to the children

Jack Who gave them to you?
Children The girl—Princess . . ., etc.
Jack (*delighted*) The Princess!!! Billy! It's the Princess! We're on our way!

Billy and Jack bring the three children up on stage—perhaps a bit of up-tempo music is played—and they go to the big shield, get the children to put their sticks in the positions. Then they shake hands with the children

Billy (*to the children*) That's just great! Here, for being such a fabulous help, you deserve some presents.

Billy produces some sweets—Mars Bars, etc., from his pocket. He and Jack hand them out to the kids as they escort them back to the stairs down to the audience

Jack } (Many thanks! We'll soon find the Princess now! } (*Speaking*
Billy } Smashing! Ta! Thanks! } *together*)
Jack (*to Billy, when the children are back in the audience*) Well, come on! I've got to find my Princess! Our friends put the gold sticks in the shield, so what happens now?

Jack and Billy go back to the big shield. Making out it is a great strain, with much groaning they manage to turn the shield on its pivot, as though a steering-wheel. Percussion effects and a dramatic chord, and either the huge pepper pot at the other wing revolves or a secret panel in the pepper pot is slid open and the Princess is revealed

The Princess steps forward

Princess (*overjoyed*) Jack!
Jack My Princess! (*He looks at the pepper pot*) Putting you in a pepper pot! What a crazy place to hide you!
Billy Oh I don't know—it's not to be sneezed at.
Princess It was so that you'd never guess where I was!
Jack (*taking her hand romantically*) Well I've found you at last! And here we are *all alone* . . .

Billy looks comically offended

Princess No-one in the world but us . . .

Billy reacts

Jack I *was* with Billy, but he knows when he's not wanted . . .

Billy reacts

Princess I thought the way he crept away without a sound was so nice.

Billy reacts

Jack And he went without being asked. Oh, my brother is a real sport.
Princess Some people get in the way, don't they—*but not your brother* . . .
Billy (*to the audience, "comedy/tragedy"*) I'm not wanted any more . . .
Princess Some people get in the way, don't they, *but not your brother* . . .

Billy exits with a comedy shrug

Audience (*probably*) Aaaah . . .

Music starts

Jack Well our friends found the golden sticks, and then I found you, and well—everything's great! (*He sings*)

Never had a dream come true

SONG 16

After the duet, Jack and the Princess exit together. Fleshcreep enters from the other side, to sinister music

Fleshcreep Jack has rescued his fair Princess
But they'll never escape, you'll see!
They've got to fight with Blunderbore
And they've got to fight with me!

The Fairy enters R

Fairy Jack will kill the Giant
When the Giant makes a blunder.
But first of all, to conquer *you*—
The Woman that's a Wonder!

The Fairy waves her wand, ushering in the Dame, and exits. The Dame enters wearing an overcoat or housecoat and a large hat

Dame (*to Fleshcreep*) Hullo, Darth Vader—(*or some other villain*)!
Fleshcreep How dare you. You'll never conquer me! I will now summon my minions!
Dame (*startled*) Pardon?
Fleshcreep Summon my minions—call out my cronies—beckon my bodyguard—EUREKA! (*He casts a spell towards both wings*)

Four minions enter, two from each side. They are either the weird animals from the opening scene of Act II or goblins, or villagers wearing sinister black domino masks over their eyes. They stand aggressively posed

(*pointing to them*) There! (*He sneers*) As for *you* conquering *me*—ha ha ha—you're very comical, my little woman.
Dame Yes I'm a woman—but *what* a woman!

She prepares herself, then turns round several times. The lights go dim, just a spotlight on her, or perhaps Strobe lighting. The "Wonderwoman" theme music is played loudly, if possible some of the cast sing the "Wonderwoman" theme into the offstage microphone. As the Dame revolves so she removes her hat and coat which she flings into the orchestra area and there she is in the Wonderwoman costume. Fleshcreep waves his arms in slow motion, encouraging his Minions to attack the Dame in turn. At a slow motion tempo in the half light with the loud Wonderwoman music and offstage singing, the Dame aims slow motion karate chops with her hands and slow motion kicks with her feet at the First, Second, Third and Fourth Minion who in turn spin away very slowly until all four or even more are spread out all over the stage. She then fights Fleshcreep downstage, clear of the others. With some grand spectacular blow she knocks him out and he falls to the floor. She puts her one booted foot on his body, arms raised above her head like a triumphant boxer. Loud chord and audience applause

(*Noticing the spread out minions*) 'Ere! You can't lie there like that! It's untidy!

She takes out a whistle and blows it

The minions all groan, stagger to their feet and exit while the Dame continues

I am the Greatest! I am Fantabulous! I am the Most! (*She looks down at Fleshcreep on the floor*) Now to throw *this* one in the castle moat! (*She bends down to drag Fleshcreep off, but she cannot pull him off, he is too heavy for her. To him*) Well come on, come on, *help* me!

The "dead" Fleshcreep puts his feet flat on the floor and makes it easier for the Dame to drag him off—a few chords to get the applause, and both exit

Fanfare, lighting change, and very dramatic music

Spick and Span enter, much scared, walking backwards, bowing towards the wings and salaaming. As they enter they give their comic salute

Spick
Span } Yes, Master! It shall be done, oh Master! { *Speaking (together)*

They face the audience, clinging to each other, and call out tremblingly

Two, four, six, eight
Who do we appreciate?
GIANT BLUNDERBORE!

Thud-thud-thud footsteps approach

The Giant enters, swinging a big spiked cudgel. If preferred, his booming voice can continue to come from the offstage microphone

Spick and Span remain scared

Giant Fee fi fo fum! Guard!
Spick Yes, your Hugeness!
Giant Bring me my golden hen!
Spick Yes, your Enormousness!

Spick scuttles away and exits on one side

Giant Guard!
Span Yes, your Massiveness!
Giant Bring me my magic harp!
Span Yes, your Colossalness!

Span exits on the other side as Spick enters holding a big hen. We hear loud cluckings on the offstage microphone

Giant Fool! Put the hen where I can watch over it—it may lay a golden egg!

Spick reaches up on tip-toe and puts the hen on the high table top. The Giant sits or stands behind the table

Span enters with the harp

Nincompoop! Put the harp where I can hear it play!

Harp music, or an imitation of it, is heard on the offstage microphone. Span reaches up and puts the harp on the high table top

Where's my food?
Spick I'll get it, your Giganticness!

Spick exits in a panic one side

Giant And where's my wine?
Span I'll get it, your Monstrosity!

Span exits in a panic on the other side while Spick returns with a plate of spaghetti—coils of white rope and laundry line on a huge plate. He reaches up and puts it on the table. Span returns with a huge golden goblet or mug and puts it up on the table, then they both stand downstage, still scared, and declaim

Spick He's colossal!
Span He's tremendous!
Spick He's gigantic!
Span He's stupendous!
Spick, **Span** He's the greatest living Giant in the world—POM—POM! (*Speaking together*)

Spick and Span do their comedy salute, and exit

The Giant "drinks" by putting the goblet to his mouth, and we hear glug—glug—glug—swallowing noises on the offstage microphone

Giant (*after the swallowing noises*) Aaaah, that was good! I like a nice drink! Whisky, brandy, vodka, and—when I want to go raving mad—some *Horlicks!* (*He lifts up the goblet and toasts the audience*) Cheers!

(*He sings a parody of the Victorian ballad "Drinking" fairly slowly and in a deep voice, especially the descending notes of the comedy coda*)

SONG 18

Oh, I like rum
Inside my tum
But I have never seen a
More perfect drink
Than a sparkling pink
Glass of good old Ribena.
I like a cup
Of Seven-Up
And Tizer gets me stinking.
Last night, my dears,
I had *ninety-eight beers*
When drinking—
Drinking—

(*He reaches the slowly sung coda*)

D-R-I-N-(*hic!*)-K-I-N-G!

(*After the song*) And another thing, Guinness Is Good For You! Ho ho ho! (*Surprised*) Ho ho! The wine has made me sleepy! But that's all right, there's no-one about. Play to me, my magic harp, play me to sleep. I'm tired.

We hear the harp effects on the offstage microphone—a tune such as "The Big Country" or similar with a reference to size

Ah, my favourite tune—(*he names the tune*). Oh—oh dear—I'm tired . . . (*He goes to sleep and snores loudly*)

Jack enters with the sword tucked in his belt. He creeps on to tingle/tension music

Jack There's old Blunderbore himself, with his singing harp and the hen that lays the golden eggs! So what the Fairy said was true! She said he always sleeps in the afternoon and he *is* sleeping. I must make certain he doesn't wake up! Maybe . . .

Tingle music continues as Jack creeps up to the front of the table, grabs the hen—immediate very loud cacklings follow on the off-stage microphone. Jack is uncertain, but he grabs the harp as well. Immediate screaming harp effects are also heard on the offstage microphone. The Giant wakes up and Jack tries to hide. He crouches near the Giant, who does not see him and puts the harp and the hen on the floor

Giant Fee fi fo fum
I smell the blood of an Englishman!

Jack nips round the table as the Giant collects his club

Be he alive or be he dead
I'll grind his bones to make my bread!

Jack Oh no, you won't!

Giant (*realizing*) AAAAH! A HORRIBLE HUMAN!

Jack I'm not afraid of you Blunderbore! You've taken all the other lads from the village, but you're not taking me!

DUEL

The Giant fights with his cudgel, Jack with the sword

Loud music plays through the action, also continuous hen and harp noises on the offstage microphone—altogether sounding like Bedlam—together with roars from the Giant and shouts from Jack

If the Giant is not very mobile, Strobe lighting can be used to help the effect. During the short fight the Giant grabs Jack's sword from him and flings it away. Jack gasps in terror, then runs to the sword and manages to collect it, all the time looking in terror at the Giant. He never takes his eyes off him, he is so scared. Jack moves close to the Giant, who merely puts his arm round him, but Jack reacts as though the Giant is crushing him to death. It appears to be a great struggle, with Jack out of breath but eventually somehow "managing to break free". Jack puts down the sword and makes use of the large-scale props such as a fork, large plate or goblet: but he hits the Giant in vain with these things—they have no effect. Finally, Jack thrusts the sword under the Giant's arm and the Giant holds it there, lets out a terrible great groan, falls over the table and is still. He is dead
Fanfare

Jack (*waving his arms above his head*) VICTORY!

The Fairy runs in and is delighted. She waves her wand to each wing, beckoning everyone on

Fairy Come on everybody! This couldn't be greater!
The Giant is as dead as a cold potater!

The King, the Dame, the Princess, Silly Billy, Clarence Clanger, Spick and Span—saluting—the Villagers—in fact all except Fleshcreep and Mrs Blunderbore enter. Daisy the Cow enters from the opposite side to the Dame, who runs over to the Cow

Dame (*emotionally, patting the Cow's head*) Oh *Daisy*, I never thought I'd see you again, etc.

Everyone sings a joyful Production Number (Song 19)—if possible getting the audience to clap in time—and marches round the stage triumphantly waving the Giant's kitchen utensils above head

At the end of the Production Number there is a Black-out

SCENE 4

DOWN TO EARTH AGAIN

In the Black-out, Billy steps forward downstage, and behind him the tabs close or the front cloth is flown in

Billy Hullo, kids!
Audience Hullo, Billy!

Billy Did you enjoy the pantomime?
Audience YES!
Billy Well so did I except for one thing. Jack's going to marry the Princess, the King's going to marry the Dame, but I'm not going to marry anybody . . .
Audience Aaaah!
Billy I know I'm not good-looking or anything like that, but I do deserve someone to love.
Audience Aaaah!
Billy Louder, I can't hear you. (*He conducts them*)
Audience Aaaah!

The Fairy enters

Fairy Because you are nice and kind and good
And you helped Jack as much as you could
I will help your romantic schemes
Behold! The girl of all your dreams!

She waves her wand

Mrs Blunderbore enters from the other side

Mrs Blunderbore (*seeing Billy and calling out rapturously*) Darling!
Billy (*to the Fairy*) Get rid of her!
Fairy Sorry! (*She calls to Mrs Blunderbore*) Away! Away!

Mrs Blunderbore exits

The Fairy quickly recites

Because you are nice and kind and good
And you helped Jack as much as you could
And because your heart is heavy laden
Here is a simple country maiden!

The Fairy waves her wand. We hear slinky music and a very seductive Girl indeed enters. The Fairy exits

Billy A simple country maiden? You've got to be joking!

To the music, the Girl slinks up to him and whispers in his ear

(*Listening*) Yes—yes—oh, fantastic! (*To the audience*) She wants to meet me in—(*comedy local place or hotel*)—after the show!

The Girl exits slinkily

(*Calling to her as she goes*) I'll be there, don't you worry! Oh, meeting her has made me feel like bursting into song. And I've got a surprise for you, you're going to burst into song as well! Now, what shall we sing . . .

Daisy the Cow enters or pops her head through the tabs, and moos

Of course, *Daisy!*

He sings and conducts the audience and the Cow sways her head in time

SONG 20

(*After the first chorus*) Lovely, give Daisy a hand! See you later, Daisy!

Daisy exits on one side and the Dame—in some easy costume change such as a coat and hat—enters from the other

Dame (*to the audience*) Just what do you think you're all doing?
Audience Singing.
Dame *Singing?* You call that singing? Sounds like water going down a plug-hole!
Billy What cheek! (*To the audience*) That's cheeky, isn't it.
Audience Yes.
Dame Oh Billy, if I had a little group of my *own* singers, we'd show you what it ought to sound like.
Billy All right then, Mum, you take that half—go on, *take* them, I don't want them!
Dame All right then, I will. Come on my lot, we'll show that other lot what a shower they are. One—two—three . . .

The Dame's side sings the chorus, while Billy takes a couple of bits of cotton wool from his pocket and stuffs them in his ears. Then his *side sings, then both sides decide to join together*

On the last notes the Dame and Billy exit waving. From other side, Clarence enters ringing the hand bell

Clarence (*proclaiming*) Everyone's invited to the wedding of Jack the Giant Killer and the Princess Melanie! (*He recites*)
Come everybody, come one and all
To the Wedding Beano at Scarlet Runner Hall!

Fanfare. The tabs open or the front cloth is flown

Scene 5

The Wedding Beano

Finale walk down. The Fairy now wears a prettier costume. Spick and Span give their last comedy salute

FINALE COUPLETS

Fleshcreep Jack climbed up the Beanstalk
Princess And he's married his Princess
Fairy And I am feeling super
'Cos at last I've changed my dress!
King I'll live happy ever after
Billy And I'll just say "God Bless"!
Jack We hope we gave you a bit of fun
That's all we claim to do
Dame And we hope that in *your* garden
You'll find a Beanstalk too!

FINAL CHORUS

(SONG 21)

FURNITURE AND PROPERTY LIST

See also Scenery Note

ACT I

Scene 1

On stage: Cottages, trees
Barrel or bucket. *In it:* flower attached to nylon thread
Milking-stool

Off stage: Large leek **(Fairy)**
Handbell **(Clarence)**
Trick sedan chair **(Spick, Span)**
Whip **(Fleshcreep)**
Drum and stick **(Billy)**
"Snow" **(Stage Management)**
Large book **(Villager)**
Catapult and ball **(Villagers)**
Milking bucket **(Billy)**
Bottle of milk, tin, toy paddle-boat **(Cow)**

Personal: **Billy:** piece of paper with poem
Dame: paper and pencil
Cow: rope, halter
Jack: book

Scene 3

On stage: As Scene 1, but decked out with flags, bunting, "Cattle Market" sign, optional fruit and vegetable stalls
Block of stone with sword in it, set under canopy
Blackboard, chalk (or could be set off, for **Spick, Span)**

Off stage: Bunches of flowers **(Gypsy Girls)**
Bucket. *In it:* backbrush, lipstick, powder puff (all outsize), straw hat with hole and ribbon, pencil, paper **(Jack)**
Stool **(Billy)**
Transparent gauze **(Dame)**
Tray with plates of coloured pie mixture **(Clarence)**
Handbell **(Clarence)**

Scene 4

On stage: 2 signposts
Tree trunk

Off stage: Bag. *In it:* gold coins, beans **(Fleshcreep)**

Scene 5

On stage: See Scenery Notes

SCENE 6

Off stage: Sword **(Fairy)**

ACT II

SCENE 1

On stage: Groundrow

Off stage: Outsize cut-out petrol tin **(Mrs Blunderbore)**

Personal: **Billy:** Dracula mask

SCENE 2

On stage: Dark-coloured chest. *In it:* 3 gold sticks

Off stage: Cut-out daisy-style flower **(Stage Management)**
Cut-out hammer **(Stage Management)**
Outsize carrot **(Stage Management)**

SCENE 3

On stage: Giant's chair
Giant's table. *On solid front:* heraldic shield on pivot with 3 clips. *Under it:* jug, baby bath with iron and large gin bottle in it
Seven-foot-high pepper pot with trick opening
Outsize hot-water bottle (can be painted on wing)
Four-foot-high fork

Off stage: Huge plates of meat, fruit, H.P. Sauce, cutlery, chain of sausages **(Villagers)**
Baby doll, with nappy and dummy **(King)**
Rattle (optional) **(Male Singer)**
4 domino masks **(Minions)**
Cudgel **(Giant)**
Large "hen" **(Spick)**
Harp **(Span)**
Giant plate of spaghetti (coils of white rope) **(Spick)**
Giant goblet **(Span)**

Personal: **Billy:** various sweets, Mars Bars, etc.
Dame: whistle

SCENE 4

Personal: **Billy:** cotton wool

SCENE 5

On stage: Rostra and stairs for walk down (optional)

EFFECTS PLOT

ACT I

Cue 1 **Jack**: "Come on, everybody, stand by!" (Page 13)
Thudding footsteps

Cue 2 **Fleshcreep** hypnotizes **Princess** (Page 25)
Thunder

Cue 3 **Fairy**: "By thunder" (2nd time) (Page 27)
Tremendous thunderclap

ACT II

Cue 4 **Mrs Blunderbore**: ". . . he will eat them!" (*Cackles*) (Page 35)
Dragon roar

Cue 5 **Fairy**: "Yes, Jack . . ." (Page 36)
Dragon roar

Cue 6 **Fairy** exits (Page 37)
Thunder, dragon roar—stop suddenly as **Dragon** *enters*

Cue 7 After **Dame, Billy** and **King** enter (Page 45)
Thudding footsteps

Cue 8 **Dame & Billy**: "You must keep it warm because. . ."
(3rd time) (Page 45)
Ear-splitting baby cries—cut with a gulp as **Billy** *inserts dummy*

Cue 9 **Billy** pours water (Page 46)
Water-pouring effect

Cue 10 **Billy**: "Well, that lukes warm." (Page 47)
Baby cries

Cue 11 **Dame** puts bottle to baby's mouth (Page 47)
Drinking noises

Cue 12 **Billy** pats baby's back (Page 47)
Loud hiccup/burp

Cue 13 **Spick & Span**; "Giant Blunderbore!" (Page 51)
Thudding footsteps

Cue 14 **Spick** enters with hen (Page 52)
Loud cluckings

Cue 15 **Giant**: ". . . where I can hear it play!" (Page 52)
Harp music, or imitation

Cue 16 **Giant** drinks (Page 52)
Swallowing noises

Cue 17 **Giant**: ". . . play me to sleep. I'm tired." (Page 53)
Harp effect—continue until **Giant** *snores*

Cue 18 **Jack** seizes hen and harp (Page 53)
Loud clucking and harp noises until **Jack** *puts both on floor*

Cue 19 During duel between **Jack** and **Giant** (Page 54)
Loud harp and hen noises

LIGHTING PLOT

Property fittings required: nil
Various front cloth and full stage settings

ACT I

Cue 1	As CURTAIN rises *Flash*	(Page 1)
Cue 2	**Fairy**: "... make you lose your mind!" *Flash*	(Page 2)
Cue 3	**Fleshcreep**: "Ow!" *Flash*	(Page 2)
Cue 4	**Fleshcreep** and **Fairy** exit *Bring up full lighting—bright sunshine*	(Page 2)
Cue 5	**Fairy** enters *Dim general lighting*	(Page 6)
Cue 6	**Fairy**: "*The sunshine.*" *Black-out, then return to previous lighting*	(Page 6)
Cue 7	**Villagers** enter *Fade up to full lighting*	(Page 7)
Cue 8	**Giant** roars *Fade general lighting*	(Page 12)
Cue 9	**Giant**'s laughter fades *Return to full lighting*	(Page 13)
Cue 10	At end of Production Number *Black-out, then up to front cloth lighting*	(Page 13)
Cue 11	**Dame**: "... an ache in my bozoom!" *Black-out, then up to full general lighting*	(Page 15)
Cue 12	**Jack** pulls sword from stone *Dim lighting to spots on* **Jack** *and* **Cow**	(Page 20)
Cue 13	**Fairy** and **Fleshcreep** exit *Return to previous lighting*	(Page 21)
Cue 14	**Dame** goes into audience *House Lights up*	(Page 23)
Cue 15	**Dame** returns to stage *Fade House Lights*	(Page 24)
Cue 16	**Fleshcreep** enters *Dim general lighting*	(Page 25)
Cue 17	**Fleshcreep** hypnotizes **Princess** *Lightning. Return to full lighting as* **King** *enters*	(Page 25)

Cue 18 All cheer at end of song reprise—optional (Page 26)
Black-out

Cue 19 **Fairy** enters (Page 26)
Flash, then bring up front cloth lighting

Cue 20 **Jack:** ". . . not United Dairies, silly!" (Page 27)
Dim lighting. Lightning flashes

Cue 21 At end of song (Page 29)
Fade to Black-out, then up to Cottage lighting, dim, evening

Cue 22 **Dame** throws beans out of window (Page 33)
Flash from garden area

Cue 23 **Fairy:** "What a day for Jack is dawning!" (Page 33)
Crossfade to Transformation lighting, then on to full Beanstalkland lighting

ACT II

To open: Full stage, rather sinister lighting

Cue 24 **Fairy** exits (Page 37)
Lightning—stop suddenly as **Dragon** *enters*

Cue 25 At end of song (Page 38)
Black-out, then up to front stage, sinister lighting

Cue 26 **Fleshcreep** exits (Page 44)
*Fade up to full interior lighting—***Giant***'s kitchen*

Cue 27 **Dame** prepares herself for battle (Page 50)
Fade lighting to spot or Strobe during fight, finishing with spot on **Dame** *in her triumph*

Cue 28 **Dame** drags **Fleshcreep** off (Page 51)
Return to full interior lighting

Cue 29 During duel of **Jack** and **Giant** (Page 54)
Strobe lighting (optional)

Cue 30 At end of Production Number (Page 54)
Black-out, then up to front cloth lighting

Cue 31 Tabs open—or front cloth rises (Page 56)
Bring up to full lighting for Finale

MADE AND PRINTED IN GREAT BRITAIN BY
LATIMER TREND & COMPANY LTD PLYMOUTH

MADE IN ENGLAND